A LEVEL Questions and Answers

ECONOMICS

Ray Powell

Chief Examiner

SERIES EDITOR: BOB McDUELL

Letts EDUCATIONAL

Contents

HOW TO USE THIS BOOK

The aim of the *Questions & Answers* series is to provide the student with the help required to attain the highest level of achievement in important examinations. This book is intended to help you with A- and AS-level Economics or, in Scotland, Higher Grade Economics. It is designed to help all students up to grade A. The series relies on the idea that an experienced Examiner can provide, through examination questions, sample answers and advice, the help a student needs to secure success. Many revision aids concentrate on providing factual information which might have to be recalled in an examination. This series, while giving factual information in an easy-to-remember form, concentrates on the other skills which need to be developed for A-level and Higher Grade examinations.

The *Questions and Answers* series is designed to provide:

- Easy-to-use **Revision Summaries** which identify important factual information. These are to remind you, in summary form, of the topics you will need to have revised in order to answer examination questions.
- Advice on the different types of question in each subject and how to answer them well to obtain the highest marks.
- Information about other skills, apart from the recall of knowledge, which will be tested in examination papers. These are sometimes called **Assessment Objectives**. Modern A-level examinations put great emphasis on the testing of other objectives apart from knowledge and understanding. Typically, questions testing these Assessment Objectives can make up over 50% of the mark allocated to written papers. Assessment Objectives include analysis, decision making, communication, problem solving, data handling, evaluation and interpretation (see p.5 for more details). The *Questions and Answers* series is intended to develop these skills by the use of questions and by showing how marks are allocated.
- Many examples of **examination questions**. Students can improve their results by studying a sufficiently wide range of questions, providing they are shown the way to improve their answers to these questions. It is advisable that students try these questions first before going to the answers and the advice which accompanies the answers. All of the questions come from actual examination papers.
- **Sample answers** to all of the questions.
- **Advice from Examiners**. By using the experience of actual Examiners, we are able to give advice which can enable students to see how their answers can be improved and success ensured.

Success in A-level examinations comes from proper preparation and a positive attitude to the examination, developed through a sound knowledge of facts and an understanding of principles. The books are intended to overcome 'examination nerves', which often come from a fear of not being properly prepared.

THE IMPORTANCE OF USING QUESTIONS FOR REVISION

Past examination questions play an important part in revising for examinations. However, it is important not to start practising questions too early. Nothing can be more disheartening than trying to do a question which you do not understand because you have not mastered the topic. Therefore, it is important to have studied a topic thoroughly before attempting any questions on it.

How can past examination questions provide a way of preparing for the examination? It is unlikely that any question you try will appear in exactly the same form on the papers you are going to take. However, the examiner is restricted on what he can set as questions must cover the whole

syllabus and test certain Assessment Objectives. The number of totally original questions you can set on any part of the syllabus is very limited and so similar ideas occur over and over again. It certainly will help you if the question you are trying to answer in an examination is familiar and you know you have done similar questions before. This is a great boost for your confidence and confidence is what is required for examination success.

Practising examination questions will also highlight gaps in your knowledge and understanding which you can go back and revise more thoroughly. It will also indicate which sorts of questions you can do well and which, if there is a choice of questions, you should avoid.

Attempting past questions will get you used to the type of language used in questions.

Finally, having access to answers, as you do in this book, will enable you to see clearly what is required by the examiner, how best to answer each question, and the amount of detail required. Attention to detail is a key aspect of achieving success at A-level.

MAXIMISING YOUR MARKS

One of the keys to examination success is to know how marks are gained and lost by candidates. There are two important aspects to this: ensuring you follow the instructions (or 'rubric') on the examination paper and understanding how papers are marked by examiners.

Often candidates fail to gain the marks they deserve because they do not follow the rubric exactly. If you are asked to answer four questions from a section and you answer five, you can only receive credit for four. The examiner may be instructed to mark the first four only and cross out additional questions. It would be unfortunate if the fifth was your best. Anyway, attempting too many questions means you will have wasted time. You cannot have spent the correct amount of time on each of the four questions and your answers could have suffered as a result.

Where a choice of questions is possible, candidates often choose the wrong questions. A question which looks familiar may not always be as easy as it seems and valuable time can be lost going up 'dead-ends'. If you have a choice, spend time reading all of the questions and making rough notes before you start. Then begin with the questions you think you can do the best and leave any you are not sure about until later when, hopefully, your confidence will have grown. When choosing, look at the marks allocated to various parts of the questions and try to judge if you are confident in those parts where most marks are available.

For every examination paper there is a mark scheme, which tells the examiner where marks should and should not be awarded. For example, where a question is worth a maximum of five marks, there will be five, six or maybe more correct marking points and the examiner will award the first five given by the candidate. A '(5)' shown after a question on an exam paper is an indication that five points are required from your answer. Obviously, lengthy writing will not gain credit unless the candidate is hitting the right responses. Try therefore to keep your answers brief and to the point. Look at your answers critically after you have written them and try to decide how many different important points you have made.

An important principle of examination marking is called consequential marking. This means that if a candidate makes a mistake, the examiner must only penalise the candidate for it once. For example, if you made a mistake early in a calculation so that you came up with an incorrect value, you would obviously lose a mark. However, if you then used this incorrect value in a later part of the question, and your working was correct apart from this incorrect value, you would not lose any more marks. Therefore, always write down all of your workings, so that you can gain marks even if you make an early slip-up.

DIFFERENT TYPES OF EXAMINATION QUESTION

The examination questions included in this book are of two types – **essay** and **data response questions** – as these are the kinds of questions most used by the examining boards.

Essay skills

Two types of essay questions are set by the various examining boards in A-level Economics: structured and unstructured. A **structured question** is divided into two parts, (a) and (b), though one or two examining boards also include questions which may have more than two parts. An **unstructured essay question** is not formally divided into separate parts, though it will usually contain more than one element and test more than one skill. Here is a typical example of an unstructured essay question:

> When, if ever, may the existence of monopoly be justified? Evaluate different ways in which the problems posed by monopoly may be reduced.

With an unstructured question, you must exercise an extra skill over and above the strictly 'economic' skills which relate to the subject matter of the question: you must judge how much time and emphasis to give to each part of the question. In the case of a structured question the total marks available are printed at the end of each part of the question; these should provide the guide on how much time to spend on each element of the question. Here is an example:

(a) How might privatisation policies be used to increase competition and reduce monopoly? (12 marks)

(b) Discuss whether the UK privatisation programme has achieved this result. (13 marks)

The examining boards have different policies on structured and unstructured questions in their essay papers. Currently, the NEAB sets only unstructured questions while, in contrast, all the questions set by the AEB are now structured into parts (a) and (b). Between these extremes, some boards such as ULEAC usually set a mix of structured and unstructured questions. Check the policy of your examining board, and make sure that you familiarise yourself with other aspects of the 'house style' of the questions – for other exam papers such as the data paper as well as for the essay paper.

Every question includes at least one key instruction, calling for example for a **discussion, explanation, assessment, evaluation, comparison** or a **contrast**. Part (a) of a structured question may very well be restricted to testing the 'lower order skills'. In this case, the key instruction may be to **describe**, **state**, **identify** or **outline**. The question may require you to describe factual information about the economy or outline or state an economic theory. The second part of a question is much more likely to require the **application of economic theory** to analyse the problem or issue posed by the first part of the question. For example, having asked you in part (a) to outline the functions of the price mechanism in a market economy, part (b) may then require you to discuss how well or badly prices may perform these functions in the housing market, or education. Look out also for the instructions to assess, evaluate or critically discuss in the second part of a structured question.

Very few essay questions can be answered simply by an uncritical historical account or by mere factual description. A principal purpose of an essay question in economics is to test whether you can introduce basic and relatively simple economic theory and analysis in a clear and reasoned way to cast light on a particular problem specified in the question. It is good practice to use the first paragraph of your answer to a question or part of a question, to define precisely the terms mentioned in the question and to state explicitly the assumptions you are making in your interpretation of the question. If you think that a question is open to more than one interpretation, then tell the examiner, and explain why you are choosing a particular interpretation. When many interpretations are possible, there is really no such thing as a 'single correct answer'. But try to get 'behind the question' to unravel its built-in assumptions and then use economic theory and analysis to

develop a coherent line of reasoning and argument. Questions asking for a **comparison** or **contrast** ought not to be answered with two separate accounts. Strictly, a comparison notes points of similarity whereas a contrast draws attention to points of difference. It is also important not to confuse questions which ask for a discussion of **causes** with those concerned with the economic **effects** resulting from a particular event or change in the economy, or from a particular government policy. When you discuss causes or effects, always remember the central importance in market economies of the price mechanism and of the concept of the margin.

Finally, a few words about diagrams and graphs. Many, and perhaps most, economic theories can be explained using one of three methods of exposition: a written account; a graph; or by means of algebra. Unless a question specifies otherwise, choose the method of exposition which you can handle most confidently and with which you feel most comfortable. Algebra has the advantages of precision and brevity, but many economics students lack confidence and sufficient practice in manipulating algebraic equations. If you engage in a long or full written account of a theory or piece of analysis, by all means introduce diagrams or graphs if they appropriately add to the explanation. However, they should complement rather than simply repeat the information you are providing in written form. Candidates often draw diagrams which fail to earn any extra marks yet which waste valuable examination time. A 'golden rule' is: if you cannot correctly remember a particular graph then leave it out. Wrongly drawn graphs serve no purpose other than to signal in the clearest possible way that you have failed to understand properly the theory you are trying to explain.

Data response skills

Data response questions usually require you to write about four or five relatively short answers based on either a **written passage of data** (from a journal or newspaper article) or **numerical data** presented in the form of a **table** or various forms of **graphs** such as line graphs, bar graphs and pie graphs.

Most of the examination boards only use data taken from 'real world' sources, though one or two boards also use made-up or simulated data. Make sure to check your board's policy. Whatever the source of the data, typically the various parts of each question become progressively more difficult. Thus the first part of a data response question may ask for a **description** of some aspect of the data or a simple **calculation**. The later parts of the question are then likely to require an explanation of one or more features of the data in terms of economic theory, and possibly an interpretation of real world events in the light of the information provided by the data.

Many of the examination techniques relevant to essay questions are also applicable to data response questions. It is perhaps even more important to read through the questions to make sure that you thoroughly understand both the data content and the questions. Make sure you study each question carefully if you have to make a choice. Avoid the temptation to elaborate your answer to a part of a question testing a 'lower order' skill, since it is unlikely that more than a couple of marks will be allocated for simple description or definition of a concept. Do not simply copy out or paraphrase the data when tackling the more demanding parts of the question which test the 'higher order' skills of explanation, evaluation and interpretation. Search for the conclusions that can reasonably be inferred from the data, and the more tentative conclusions that really require stronger supporting evidence than that provided by the data alone. Sometimes a question will explicitly ask for a statement of the assumptions upon which the arguments in the data are based or upon which you are making your interpretation. It may also ask for a discussion of other sources of information or data that might allow you to draw stronger inferences or conclusions. You should try to learn the skill of showing the examiner when you are drawing conclusions based solely on the data in the question, and when you are bringing in 'outside information', either in the form of economic theory or descriptive fact, to help in its interpretation.

As mentioned, numerical data questions may be based on various forms of statistical data such as **tabulated schedules**, **charts** and **different types of graph**. Data questions aim to test economic knowledge rather than calculation alone, so when a calculation is required, an arithmetic slip

should not be heavily penalised provided that you have clearly shown that you are using the correct economic method to answer the question.

Time-series data, which measure changes in economic variables such as national income, output and expenditure, usually fluctuate both **seasonally** and **cyclically** with the upswings and downswings of the **business cycle**. Great care should be taken when interpreting a short annual time-series of less than ten years. With such data it is easy to confuse the long-term trend of the data with relatively short-term fluctuations associated with the business cycle. As a general rule, time-series data must extend over more than one business cycle to allow a long-term trend to be detected. Where it is possible to detect a long-term trend from the data, it may be possible to extrapolate the trend in order to **predict** or **forecast** the future. But beware however, of basing a forecast of the future upon data subject to violent fluctuations, and always be prepared for the possibility of a **structural change** or 'outside shock' occurring in the future which may upset the forecast. And even when the long-term trend is estimated, for example by measuring changes in the economy from peak to peak in succeeding business cycles, there is always the possibility that structural changes taking place within the economy have caused the underlying trend to alter. Seasonal fluctuations are not of course shown in annual data, but they should be evident in monthly and quarterly data, unless the data have already been adjusted to get rid of the seasonal fluctuations. **Seasonally adjusted data** are better for displaying the long-term trend from year to year whereas **unadjusted data** show the fluctuations from season to season within each year in the data series.

Many economic variables measured in money units are affected by inflation, which can seriously distort time-series data. Check whether data are unadjusted for inflation, in which case the data is presented in the **current prices** of each year in the data series, or whether the data have been either converted into the **constant prices** of a particular year in the series, or expressed as **index numbers**. When data is presented in index number form, the number 100 is used to represent the base year. Percentages must of course add up to 100, so there is an obvious danger of misinterpreting index numbers as percentages, and vice versa. Current price data unadjusted to get rid of the effects of inflation, is also called **nominal data**, whereas constant price data or data in index number form is known as **real data**. Finally, don't ignore basic skills, such as identifying the units being used, checking the axes on graphs and reading headings and sources of data.

ASSESSMENT OBJECTIVES

These are the skills you will be tested on through the examination questions. You will be expected to:

- Demonstrate knowledge and understanding of economic principles, theories, concepts and models in order to understand current economic issues and economic processes at work in the UK, European Union and global economies;
- Detect logical fallacies in argument, recognise unstated assumptions, distinguish between statements of fact, statements of value and hypothetical statements;
- Apply economic concepts and principles to help analyse economic issues;
- Select relevant data, demonstrate knowledge and understanding of such data, interpret data in a variety of written, graphical and numerical forms;
- Identify and investigate economic problems; analyse, discuss and critically evaluate economic ideas, arguments, proposals and policies, taking into account relevant data and theory;
- Organise and present material and arguments in a concise, logical and relevant way, and communicate clearly and accurately, taking into account the use of grammar, punctuation and spelling;
- Assess economic arguments and evidence and make informed judgements.

1 Economic systems and the market mechanism

REVISION SUMMARY

Economic systems and the 'economic problem'

An **economic system** is the set of institutions within which a community decides such questions as **what**, **how** and for **whom** to produce. Sometimes, economic systems are classified in terms of who owns the means of production. Here the main distinction is between **capitalism**, based on private ownership, and **socialism** or state ownership.

Market economies and command economies

Perhaps the most widely used method of defining and classifying economic systems is according to the **allocative mechanism** by which scarce resources reach the people who eventually consume or use them. The two allocative mechanisms by which economic systems are defined are the **market mechanism** (or **price mechanism**) and the **command mechanism** (or **planning mechanism**). An economic system in which goods and services are purchased through the price mechanism in a system of markets is called a **market economy**, whereas one in which government officials or planners allocate economic resources to firms and other productive enterprises is called a **command economy** (or planned economy). Since the breakup in the early 1990s of the Soviet Union and its 'client states' in central and eastern Europe, there are few command economies left in the world economy.

Mixed economies

A **mixed economy**, as the name suggests, is a mixture of different types of economic system. A mixed economy is intermediate between a market economy and a command economy, containing large market and non-market sectors. In terms of ownership of the means of production, a mixed economy contains large public and private sectors.

Markets

A **market** is a meeting of buyers and sellers in which goods or services are exchanged for other goods or services. For a market to operate efficiently: (i) individual buyers and sellers must decide what, how, how much, where and when to trade or exchange; (ii) they must do so with reference to their self-interest and to the alternatives or opportunities open to them; the exchange must be voluntary; if one party forces a transaction upon the other, it is not a market transaction; (iii) prices convey to the market participants information about self-interest and opportunities; for a market to allocate resources between different types of activity and to co-ordinate the activities of the separate but interdependent units that make up an economy, **prices must respond to the forces of supply and demand**.

The functions of prices

In a market economy, prices perform three main functions:

- **The signalling function –** Prices signal what is available, conveying the information which allows all the traders in the market to plan and co-ordinate their economic activities.
- **The incentive function –** Prices create incentives for **'economic agents'** (for example **households** and **firms**) to behave and make decisions in ways consistent with pursuing and achieving the fulfilment of their self-interest.
- **The rationing function –** When buyers and sellers in the market must respond to the incentives provided by the price mechanism, society's scarce resources are rationed or allocated between competing uses.

Demand and supply curves

A market can be represented by a **demand curve** and a **supply curve**, which map the **market plans** or **intended market behaviour** of households and firms. In the diagram opposite, the demand curve D_1 shows the quantities of a good the households would like to purchase at different prices. This is called **planned demand** or **intended demand**. Similarly, the supply curve S_1 shows

how much the firms would like to supply at different prices. This is **planned supply** or **intended supply**.

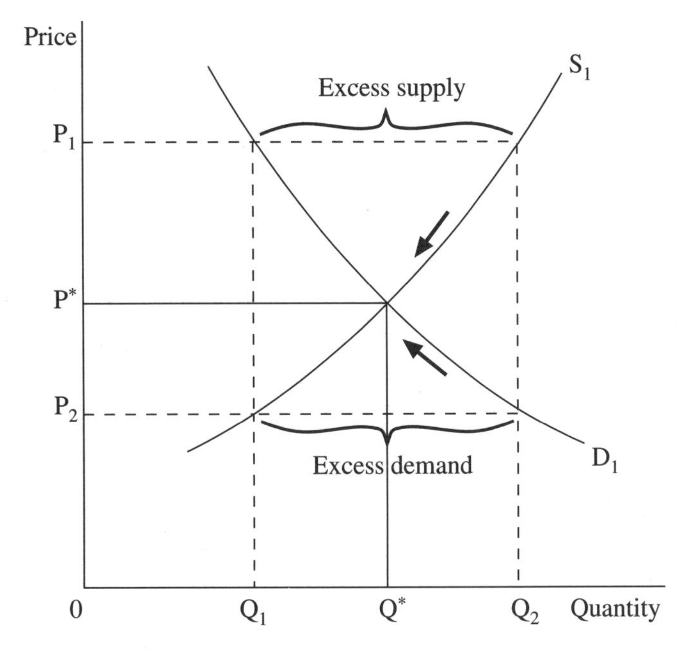

The market mechanism and the equilibrium price

How the price mechanism brings about market equilibrium

The concepts of **equilibrium** and **disequilibrium** are of very great importance in economics. Equilibrium should be regarded as a **state of rest** in which an economic agent, such as a household or firm, is **able to fulfil its market plans**. Conversely, a state of disequilibrium exists when **market plans are not fulfilled or realised**. In the supply and demand diagram, P_1 is a disequilibrium price because the firms cannot fulfil their plans at this price, i.e. *planned supply exceeds planned demand*, and there is **excess supply** in the market at this price. When there is excess supply, firms react to the stocks of unsold goods which accumulate at this price by accepting a lower price. Eventually the price falls to the equilibrium price P* at which the amount the households wish to buy equals exactly the quantity firms are prepared to supply. Likewise, when there is **excess demand**, as at price P_2, households bid up the price to P*. The equilibrium price P* is thus the only price which satisfies both households and firms, who consequently have no reason to change their market plans. At P*, the amount households intend to buy equals the quantity firms plan to supply or sell and the market clears. **Market equilibrium** only occurs when **planned demand = planned supply**.

Shifts of demand and supply

Market disequilibrium initially arises as a result of a *shift* of either the demand curve or the supply curve. When we draw a demand curve, we assume that all the other variables which may also influence planned demand are held unchanged or constant. These other variables, which include disposable income and tastes or fashion, are known as the **conditions of demand**. Likewise, the variables which fix the position of the supply curve, which include costs of production incurred by firms and taxes levied upon firms by the government, are called the **conditions of supply**.

The diagram overleaf illustrates a rightward shift of demand, resulting perhaps from a successful advertising campaign for a product.The demand curve shifts rightwards (or upwards) from D_1 to D_2. Conditions of supply have not changed, so the supply curve remains at S_1. As a result, P_1 is no longer an equilibrium price: at this price consumers demand Q_3, but firms restrict supply to Q_1. The market mechanism now swings into action to eliminate the excess demand that

REVISION SUMMARY

exists in the market at this price. The price rises until a new equilibrium is established at P_2, where the new demand curve D_2 intersects the original supply curve S_1. The equilibrium quantity is now Q_2.

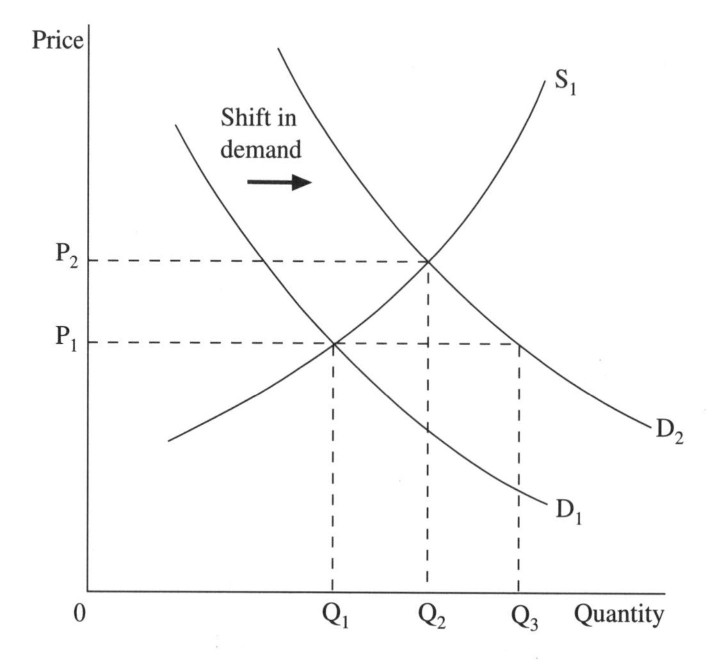

The adjustment to a new equilibrium following a shift in demand

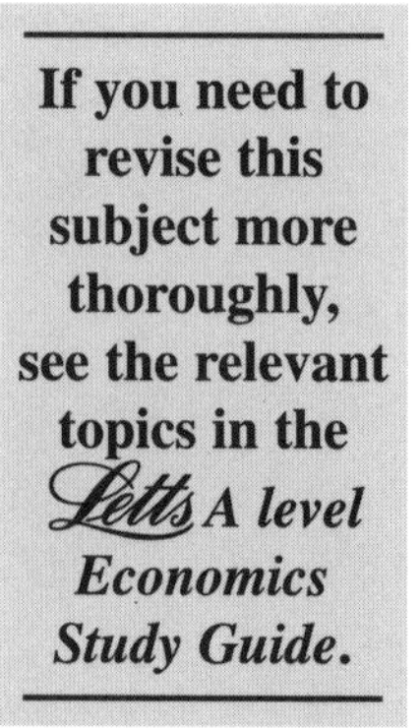

QUESTIONS

1 (a) How are resources allocated in a mixed economy? (15)

(b) In the light of the changes that have occurred in the structure of the United Kingdom economy in recent years, discuss whether it is still correct to describe the United Kingdom economy as a mixed economy. (10)

AEB

2 (a) Explain the functions that prices perform in a market economy. (12)

(b) Assess the case for and against using the price mechanism to relieve the problem of traffic congestion. (13)

AEB

3 (a) How do the forces of demand and supply determine price in a free market? (7)

(b) Explain why the demand for a product tends to rise as its price falls. (6)

(c) Identify the factors, other than price, which affect the demand for a product. Use appropriate examples and discuss how important these "non-price" factors are in determining the demand for a product. (12)

SEB

Market structures and economic welfare

A fundamental purpose of any economic system should be to achieve the highest possible state of human happiness or welfare. Within a market economy, the market structures of **perfect competition**, **imperfect competition** and **monopoly** must therefore ultimately be judged according to the extent to which they contribute to improving human happiness and well-being.

The meaning of economic efficiency

Any economic decision or course of action (by an individual, a firm or the government) is efficient if it achieves the economic agent's desired objective with minimum undesired side-effects or distortion. In this sense, efficiency is one of the canons or principles of taxation, providing a criterion (along with other canons such as economy, equity, etc.) which is used to judge how well or badly a tax performs.

Different types of economic efficiency

In order to judge the contribution of a market structure to human welfare, we must first assess the extent to which the market structure is **efficient** or **inefficient**. There are a number of different efficiency concepts which economists use. These include: (i) **technical efficiency**; (ii) **productive efficiency** (or **cost efficiency**); (iii) **X-efficiency**; (iv) **allocative efficiency**; (v) **Pareto efficiency**; (vi) **static efficiency**; and (vi) **dynamic efficiency**. Some of these efficiency concepts have quite distinctive meanings, but with others there is a certain amount of overlap which can cause confusion for students.

Technical efficiency

Production is a process of converting inputs (or 'factors of production') into outputs. A production process is **technically efficient** if it produces the largest possible output of a good from a given or available set of inputs. Alternatively, we can say that for a particular level of output, a production process is technically efficient if it minimises the inputs of capital and labour required to produce that level of output.

Productive efficiency

Technical efficiency is very closely related to the concept of **productive efficiency** (or **cost efficiency**) and sometimes they are treated as being the same. Technical efficiency, as defined above, is measured purely in terms of a technical relationship in production – often an engineering relationship – between inputs and outputs. By contrast, since productive efficiency (or cost efficiency) is measured in terms of money costs of production, it is affected by the cost or price paid for factors of production as well as by the technical relationship between inputs and outputs. Productive efficiency requires that any size of output must be produced at the lowest possible average money cost. And, comparing all plant sizes, the most productively efficient of all a firm's possible levels of output is produced at the optimum plant size and at the lowest point on the firm's long run average cost curve, where unit costs are minimised.

X-efficiency

X-inefficiency, which is an application of the concepts of technical and productive inefficiency, occurs whenever, for any particular scale of fixed capacity and level of production, the firm incurs unnecessary production costs, i.e. it could in principle reduce costs. A firm can be X-inefficient in one of two ways. Firstly, at any level of output, the firm may fail to combine its factors of production in a technically efficient way. 'Overmanning' and continuously idle machinery provide evidence of X-inefficiency. Secondly, X-inefficiency may be caused by the firm paying its workers or managers unnecessarily high wages or salaries, or buying its raw materials or capital at unnecessarily high prices. If we define an average cost curve as showing the lowest possible unit costs a firm can incur when producing different levels of output, it follows that all points on the cost curve are **X-efficient** and all points off or above the cost curve are X-inefficient.

REVISION SUMMARY

Allocative efficiency

An economy is said to be **allocatively efficient** when it is impossible to improve total welfare by reallocating productive resources between markets and industries. More specifically, allocative efficiency occurs when **P = MC** in all the industries and markets of the economy. You should read the answer to the first question at the end of this unit for a detailed explanation of the concept.

Other efficiency concepts

In a productive sense, an economy is said to be **Pareto-efficient** if it is impossible to increase the output of one good without reducing the output of some other good. This implies that all the economy's available resources or factors of production are fully employed and that all goods are being produced in a technically efficient way. In an allocative sense, an economy is Pareto-efficient if it is impossible to make one person better off without making another individual worse off, implying that a state of allocative efficiency has been attained. All the efficiency types which we have considered so far, are forms of **static efficiency**. They ignore the fact that the economy is constantly changing, with new technologies, methods of production and final goods being developed and economic growth taking place. By contrast with static efficiency, **dynamic efficiency** results from improvements in technical and productive efficiency that occur over time. A dynamically efficient economy is one which is proficient at improving methods of producing existing products, and also at developing and marketing completely new products. In both cases, invention, innovation and research and development (R&D) can lead to significant improvements in dynamic efficiency.

If you need to revise this subject more thoroughly, see the relevant topics in the *Letts A level Economics Study Guide*.

QUESTIONS

1 'In order to achieve maximum economic efficiency, the market price of a commodity must equal the marginal cost of the product.'

(a) Describe the market structure in which the above condition always exists. Show how this market structure is advantageous to consumers of that product. (14)

(b) Describe one market structure in which this condition does not apply and explain how efficiency and equity may be impaired. (16)

SEB

2 (a) Analyse the conditions of profit maximisation for a firm operating under conditions of absolute monopoly. (8)

(b) On what basis is the control of monopoly thought to be desirable? (12)

UCLES

3 *Competition and innovation in the European Community*

There are a number of obstacles which restrict trade within the European Community, and there are good reasons to think that removing them may bring substantial gains to all member states. Policies have been suggested to tackle these problems, and if they are adopted they are likely to improve the allocation of
5 resources within the European Community.

The primary effects of reducing the barriers to trade between countries who are members of the European Community will be an increase in market size and in the amount of competition in the enlarged market. These changes are likely to affect the efficiency of firms and the performance of markets in different ways. When
10 examining these effects, it is necessary to distinguish between dynamic efficiency and static efficiency.

Improvements in dynamic efficiency will result if the removal of barriers to trade leads to invention, innovation and a faster rate of technological change. However, even if these long-run benefits do not occur it is still almost certain that there will be
15 improvements in static efficiency.

A larger market and the resulting increase in demand will allow firms with unexploited economies of scale to move down their long-run average cost curves. More competition is also likely to encourage firms to reduce inefficiency and to produce whatever output they choose, at the lowest average cost. These two effects lead to the prediction that costs are likely to fall as the size of the market and the degree of competition increase. 20

The effects of market size and competition on dynamic efficiency, however, are much less clear. Certainly it seems reasonable to suggest that increases in market size will increase innovation, particularly if there are any economies of scale or fixed costs in the research and development process. However, the effect of competition on innovation is rather more controversial. Some economists believe that large firms with at least some degree of monopoly power are likely to be the most innovative. If this is true, it is not certain that removing barriers to trade between the members of the European Community will improve dynamic efficiency. Indeed, it is possible that the static efficiency gains will be more than outweighed by losses arising from a reduction in dynamic efficiency. 25 30

Source: Adapted from *Competition and Innovation* by G.A. Geroski: an internal economic paper for the Commission of the European Communities.

(a) Explain, in your own words, what the writer means by the terms:

(i) dynamic efficiency (line 10) (2)

(ii) static efficiency (line 11) (2)

(iii) monopoly power (line 27). (2)

(b) Explain why it seems reasonable to argue that:

(i) 'increases in market size will increase innovation' (lines 23–24). (5)

(ii) 'large firms with at least some degree of monopoly power are likely to be the most innovative' (lines 26–27). (5)

(c) Discuss the view that removing all barriers to trade within the European Community will bring substantial gains to all member states. (9)

AEB

3 Competitive strategies in oligopolistic markets

REVISION SUMMARY

The meaning of oligopoly

Oligopoly, which is sometimes called **'imperfect competition amongst the few'**, exists when there are just a few firms in the market (or just a few *dominant* firms). However, oligopoly is best defined by **market conduct**, or the **behaviour of the firms** within the market, rather than by the precise number of firms in the market and the degree of market concentration. For example, the effect upon profits of a price change undertaken by an oligopolist depends upon the **likely reactions of the other firms**; so when deciding a price strategy, an oligopolist must make some assumptions about the likely response of the other firms. Oligopoly is characterised by **reactive market behaviour** and by **interdependence between firms**, rather than by the independent choice of price or output which is assumed to exist in the other market structures.

Perfect and imperfect oligopoly

Perfect oligopoly is said to exist when the oligopolists produce a uniform or homogeneous product, such as petrol. By contrast, an **imperfect oligopoly** exists when the products produced by the oligopoly are by their nature differentiated, for example automobiles.

Competitive and collusive oligopoly

Competitive oligopoly exists when the rival firms are *interdependent* in the sense that they must take account of the reactions of one another when forming a market strategy, but *independent* in the sense that they **decide the market strategy without co-operation or collusion**. The existence of uncertainty is a characteristic of competitive oligopoly; a firm can never be completely certain of how rivals will react to its marketing strategy. If the firm raises its price, will the rivals follow suit or will they hold their prices steady in the hope of gaining sales and market share? Uncertainty can be reduced and perhaps eliminated by the rivals **co-operating** or **colluding** to fix prices or output in a **cartel agreement**, or even by allocating customers to particular members of the oligopoly.

Price competition and other forms of competition

When firms collectively agree to fix the market in conditions of collusive oligopoly, prices are of course likely to be stable. Evidence also suggests that prices are very often relatively stable in competitive oligopoly as well as when the firms can collude or co-operate with each other. Even though no formal – or even informal – collective pricing agreement exists, firms realise that a **price war** will be self-defeating for all the firms involved. They therefore may reach a tacit understanding not to indulge in aggressive price competition as a means of gaining extra profits or market share at the expense of each other. In the absence of keen price competition, oligopolistic firms are likely to undertake forms of non-price competition, such as: (i) **marketing competition**, including obtaining **'exclusive outlets'** such as tied petrol stations through which oil companies can sell their products; (ii) the use of **persuasive advertising**, **product-differentiation**, **brand-imaging** and **packaging**; (iii) **quality competition**, including the **provision of after-sale service**.

The kinked demand curve theory of oligopoly

This theory was originally developed to explain alleged price rigidity and the absence of price wars in oligopolistic markets. Suppose that an oligopolist produces the output Q_1 illustrated in the diagram opposite, selling his output at price P_1. The demand curve DD has been drawn on the assumption that the firm *expects* that demand for its product will be **relatively elastic in response to a price rise** because rivals are expected to react by keeping their prices stable in the hope of gaining profits and market share. Conversely, the oligopolist expects his rivals to react to a price cut by decreasing their prices by an equivalent amount; he therefore expects demand to be **relatively inelastic in response to a decision to reduce price**, since he cannot hope to lure many customers away from his rivals. The oligopolist therefore expects his rivals to react asymmetrically when price is raised compared to when price is lowered. As a result, he believes his initial price and output at point A to be at the junction of two demand curves of different

elasticity, each reflecting a different assumption about how rivals are expected to react to a change in price. The oligopolist expects that profits may be lost whether the price is raised or cut. On these assumptions, the best policy is to leave price unchanged!

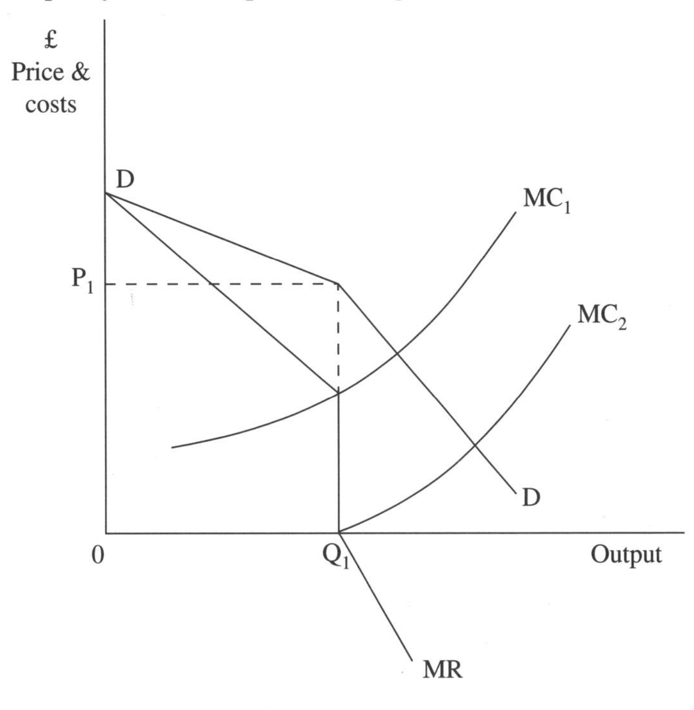

The 'kinked' demand curve theory of oligopoly

There is also a second reason why prices may tend to be stable in conditions of ‘kinked’ demand. A mathematical discontinuity exists along a vertical line above output Q_1, between the marginal revenue curves associated respectively with the relatively elastic and relatively inelastic demand (or average revenue) curves. The marginal cost curve can rise or fall within the range of this discontinuity, without altering the profit-maximising output Q_1 or price P_1. If marginal costs rise above MC_1 or fall below MC_2, the profit maximising output changes and the oligopolist must set a different price to maximise profits, assuming of course that the curve DD accurately represents the correct demand curve facing the firm. But the oligopolist’s selling price remains stable as long as the marginal cost curve lies between MC_1 and MC_2.

Other aspects of oligopoly pricing

- **Cost-plus pricing –** simply means that a firm sets its selling price by adding a standard percentage profit margin to average or unit costs.
- **Price parallelism –** occurs when there are identical prices and price movements within an industry or market. It is worth noting that price parallelism can be caused by two completely opposite sets of circumstances. On the one hand, price parallelism would occur in a very competitive market, approximating to perfect competition, as the firms adjusted to a ruling market price determined by demand and supply in the market as a whole. But on the other hand, price parallelism results from price leadership in tightly oligopolistic industries.
- **Price leadership –** Because overt collusive agreements to fix the market price, such as cartel agreements, are usually made illegal by government, oligopolistic firms use less formal or tacit ways to co-ordinate their pricing decisions. An example of **covert collusion** is price leadership, which occurs when one firm becomes the market leader and other firms in the industry follow its pricing example.
- **Price discrimination –** occurs when firms charge different prices to different customers based on differences in the customers’ ability and willingness to pay. Those customers who are

REVISION SUMMARY

prepared to pay more are charged a higher price than those who are only willing to pay a lower price. It is important to note that the different prices charged are not based on any differences in costs of production or supply.

- **Limit pricing –** The central assumption of the 'limit pricing' theory is that established firms in the market set their prices taking into account the effect they may have on long-run profitability by possibly attracting new firms into the industry who would erode their monopoly power. Firms may decide to set prices which, by deterring the entry of new firms, act as a **barrier to entry**. Thus the established firms sacrifice the short-term maximised profits which higher prices would yield in order to maximise long-run profits, achieved through preventing or limiting the entry of new firms.
- **Predatory pricing –** Whereas limit pricing deters market entry, successful predatory pricing removes recent entrants to the market. Predatory pricing occurs when an established firm deliberately sets prices below costs to force new market entrants out of business. Once the new entrants have left the market, the established firm will usually restore prices to their previous level.

If you need to revise this subject more thoroughly, see the relevant topics in the Letts *A level Economics Study Guide*.

QUESTIONS

1 (a) Explain why firms in a certain industry may wish to collude with each other in setting prices in a cartel agreement. (10)

(b) Why might collusion between firms be held to be against the 'public interest'? (10)

(c) For what reasons has it been asserted that collusive agreements often tend to break down in the long run? (5)

WJEC

2 (a) Carefully explain why a firm may charge different prices for the same product. (15)

(b) Discuss whether such a pricing policy is in the interest of the firm's customers. (10)

AEB

3 Study the data below and answer the questions which follow.

Early in 1994, a few months before the opening of the Channel Tunnel to passenger traffic, the prices shown in Table 1 were announced by the main cross-Channel operators for the summer and winter months in 1994/95. The passage in Extract A has been adapted from a newspaper article published at the time.

Table 1

Return Standard Fares: Dover or Folkestone to Calais, Car plus Passengers

	Winter off-peak	Summer off-peak	Summer peak weekend
Le Shuttle (operated by Eurotunnel)	£220	£280	£310
Stena Sealink car ferry	£126	£220	£320
P&O car ferry	£139	£139–£221	£289–£320
Hoverspeed hovercraft ferry	£142	£297	£338

Source: *The Independent*, 12 January 1994

Extract A

'The market from which Eurotunnel needs to carve itself a share is perhaps 20 million a year. The company has suggested that, by 1996, it might be carrying 8 million car passengers. But this makes a huge assumption: it assumes that ferry prices will not be slashed in order to try to win back some of the 8 million people who have gone underground. But ferry prices are bound to fall – the real cost of crossing the Channel has been falling by 3 or 4 per cent annually for years. 5

Eurotunnel insisted yesterday that it's not interested in a price war with the ferries. Instead, it feels that it can attract sufficient takers by promising a 35-minute crossing time with no weather hold-ups and no seasickness. When Eurotunnel opens there is going to be a vast increase in cross-Channel capacity for people, cars and freight. But 10 if there is no price war, there is little reason to think that there will be any large increase in the volume of traffic carried. In other words, the total revenue to be divided up between the rival operators will not be greatly different from today's. And what if there is a price war? The volume of traffic may well increase as more people will be tempted to cross the Channel. But because each crossing is at a lower average 15 price for the operator – be it a ferry operator or Eurotunnel – the total amount of money will not go up as steeply as the traffic volume.'

Adapted from 'Tunnel tariffs won't add up when the novelty wears off' by Ben Laurance, *The Guardian*, 12 January 1994

(a) What market structure amongst cross-Channel travel operators is suggested by the data? Explain your reasons. (3)

(b) Explain why the cross-Channel travel operators charge different prices at peak and off-peak travel times as shown in Table 1. (6)

(c) In the light of the information in the data, discuss whether it is realistic for Eurotunnel to aim for a market of 8 million car passengers by 1996. (Lines 2–3 Extract A) (13)

(d) In January 1994, Eurotunnel stated that the company was 'not interested in a price war with the ferries'. (Line 7 in Extract A). Taking account of both short-run and long-run factors, evaluate the case that it would not be in the interest of the cross-Channel travel operators to engage in a price war. (13)

AEB

4 Economies of scale and industrial change

REVISION SUMMARY

The meaning of economies of scale

Economies of scale occur when a firm's long-run average production costs fall as a result of an increase in the scale of production. **Internal economies of scale** result from an increase in the size of the firm itself or of an increase in the size of a plant or plants operated by the firm. By contrast a firm benefits from **external economies of scale** when unit production costs fall because of the growth of the scale of the whole industry rather than of the firm itself.

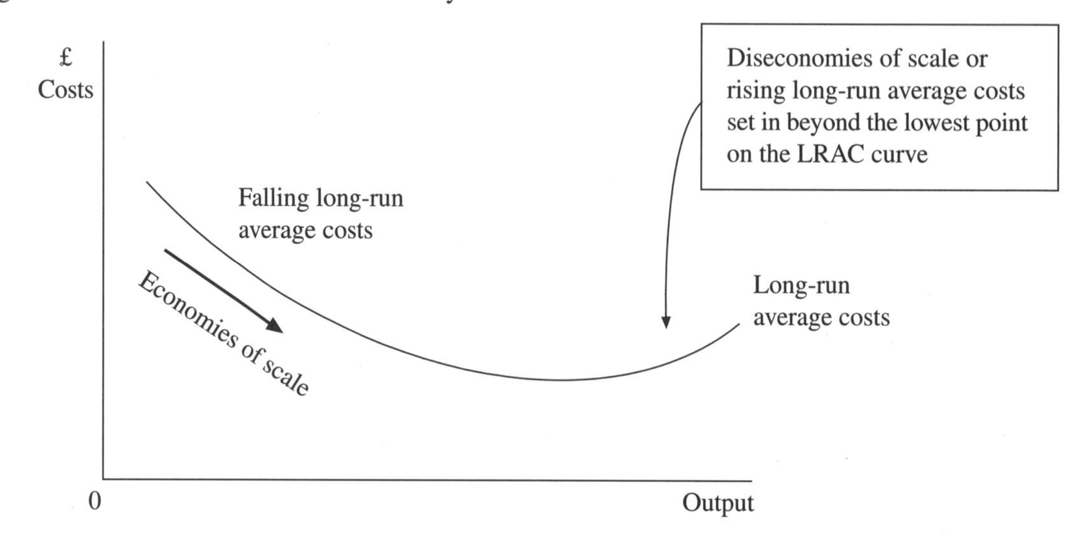

Returns to scale

Economies and diseconomies of scale are closely related to increasing and decreasing returns to scale. If an increase in the scale of all the factors of production (in the economic long run) causes a more than proportionate increase in output, the firm is said to be benefiting from **increasing returns to scale**. These result in falling long-run average costs, and hence in economies of scale. However, constant returns to scale and decreasing returns to scale are also possible. **Constant returns to scale**, which result in constant long-run average costs, occur when an increase in the scale of all the factors of production causes a proportionate increase in output. Finally, **decreasing returns to scale** result when an increase in the scale of all the factors of production causes a less than proportionate increase in output, leading to rising long-run average costs or diseconomies of scale.

Plant-level economies of scale

It is useful to distinguish between those internal economies of scale that occur at the level of a single plant or establishment owned by a firm and those occurring at the level of the firm itself. **Plant-level economies of scale** are largely **technical economies of scale**, though some management economies are also possible at plant level. The main types of technical economy of scale are:

- **indivisibilities or 'lumpiness' –** Many types of plant or machinery are indivisible in the sense that there is a certain minimum size below which they cannot efficiently operate.
- **the spreading of research and development costs –** With large plants R&D costs can be spread over a much longer production run, reducing unit costs in the long run.
- **volume economies –** These are also known as **economies of increased dimensions**. With many types of capital equipment (for example metal smelters, transport containers, storage tanks and warehouses), costs increase less rapidly than capacity.
- **economies of massed resources –** The operation of a number of identical machines in a large plant means that proportionately less spare parts need be kept than when fewer machines are involved. It is unlikely that all the machines will develop a fault at the same time.

REVISION SUMMARY

- **economies of vertically-linked processes –** The linking of processes in a single plant – from the initial purchase of raw materials, components and energy through to the completion and sale of the finished product – can lead to a saving in time, transport costs and energy; and the close proximity of specialist workshops within the plant may allow a subsequent stage in the production process to obtain exactly the right supplies in the right quantity and at the right time.

Managerial economies of scale can be achieved both by increasing the size of an individual plant or, at the level of the firm, by grouping a larger number of establishments under one management.

Firm-level economies of scale

Businesses will also try to take advantage of any scale economies associated with the growth of the enterprise that are largely independent of plant size. **Economies of scale at the firm level** arise from the firm itself being large rather than from operating a single big plant or a number of large plants. As well as covering some of the R&D economies, massed resources economies and managerial economies already described, firm-level economies of scale include:

- **marketing economies –** These are of two types: **bulk-buying** and **bulk-marketing** economies.
- **financial or capital-raising economies of scale –** The **bulk-borrowing** of funds required to finance the business's expansion.
- **risk-bearing economies of scale –** Large firms are usually less exposed to risk than small firms, because risks can be grouped and spread.

Industrialisation and deindustrialisation

Industrialisation can be defined as the growth of manufacturing, factory production and the secondary sector, and in the process of industrialisation, the secondary or manufacturing sector grows to become the largest and dominant sector of the economy. By contrast, **deindustrialisation** refers to the structural decline of manufacturing output in the face of international competition. Some use the term to refer only to the **absolute decline** of manufactured output which occurred in the severe recessions of the early 1980s and 1990s. If defined in this way, then deindustrialisation has only occurred in the downturn and recessionary stages of the business cycle. In 1995, the UK economy entered into its third year of economic recovery with both GDP and manufacturing output growing steadily. But if the term is used in a *relative* sense, describing the decline of manufacturing relative to the service sector, deindustrialisation has been occurring continuously for decades, and it continues despite the recovery in manufacturing output which takes place between periods of recession. 'Deindustrialisation' can also be extended beyond *manufacturing* industry to encompass the relative or absolute decline of extractive industries, such as coal mining and fisheries, and possibly the construction and utility industries. Although defined in terms of industrial *output*, deindustrialisation has been accompanied by an often rapid fall in industrial *employment.*

Does deindustrialisation matter?

Many free-market economists argue that the deindustrialisation taking place in the UK economy has not in itself been a problem and need not be the cause of other problems. They believe that manufacturing industries are not intrinsically superior to service industries. Indeed, very often the dirty, dangerous, and routine circumstances in which much factory production takes place make manufacturing a much less pleasant environment in which to work than the service sector. Keynesian economists do not usually accept the view that 'manufacturing does not matter'. They argue that in an advanced economy a strong and competitive manufacturing base is needed for two main reasons: firstly, only manufacturing can yield the long-run growth in productivity or output per worker necessary for continued improvement in living standards; and secondly, manufactured goods can be exported and substituted for imports, whereas many services cannot, making a competitive manufacturing sector necessary if the British economy is to pay its way in the world.

If you need to revise this subject more thoroughly, see the relevant topics in the *Letts A level Economics Study Guide.*

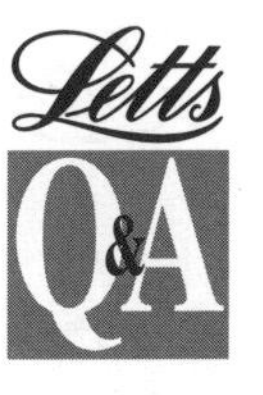

QUESTIONS

1 If economies of scale are so significant, why are there so many small firms in the economy? (25)

AEB

2 (a) How might the decline in the relative importance of manufacturing industry in the UK economy since 1979 be explained? (70)

(b) Should the government wish to halt this decline, examine the measures which could be used. (30)

ULEAC

3 *Output and Employment change in Manufacturing Industry in Great Britain 1971–1983*

Deindustrialisation in the British economy has been taking place over many years. It is, however, generally accepted by economists that the pace of deindustrialisation was particularly marked from around 1970 to the mid-1980s, after which the relative rate of deindustrialisation slowed down. The table below shows output and employment changes for the main manufacturing sectors in this period.

	1971–83	
	Output change (%)	*Employment change (%)*
Food, drink and tobacco	+12.0	–22.8
Coal and petroleum products	–22.3	–47.6
Chemicals and allied industries	+26.6	–16.2
Metal manufacturing	–33.6	–53.4
Mechanical engineering	–23.6	–35.9
Instrument engineering	+7.3	–24.7
Electrical engineering	+45.3	–21.4
Shipbuilding and marine engineering	–25.6	–28.8
Vehicles	–21.0	–36.0
Other metal goods	–32.3	–30.6
Textiles	–38.3	–50.8
Leather goods and fur	–42.7	–40.9
Clothing and footwear	–12.9	–41.2
Bricks, pottery, glass, cement	–16.3	–36.1
Timber, furniture	–11.5	–22.8
Paper, printing and publishing	–4.1	–19.5
Other manufacturing	–0.2	–31.5
All manufacturing	–8.3	–32.2

(a) (i) Which industry has experienced the largest change in employment during this period? (1)

(ii) What additional information would you require in order to say whether it has experienced the largest number of job losses? (2)

(b) (i) How can changes in productivity be derived from this data? (2)

(ii) In which manufacturing industry has productivity
– increased most of all?
– fallen in real terms?
Justify your answers. (4)

(c) (i) Compare the output and employment changes in vehicles and textiles over this period. (2)

(ii) State and explain two likely reasons which might account for the variation. Justify your answers. (4)

(d) Explain what other information you would require in order to make a full assessment of the costs and benefits of deindustrialisation in Britain from 1971 to 1983. (5)

UCLES

The meaning of privatisation

Privatisation can be defined as the transfer of publicly-owned assets to the private sector. In the UK this has usually involved the sale to private ownership of industries and businesses (called **nationalised industries**) which were previously owned by the state and accountable to central government. Although the main privatisations have involved the sale of nationalised industries, other state-owned assets such as land and council houses have also been privatised.

The main privatisations in the UK

Since 1979, the Conservative Government has transferred over two dozen publicly-owned enterprises into the private sector. The main privatisations, and the year in which they took place, are shown in the following table:

British Aerospace	1981	British Airports Authority	1987
National Freight Corporation	1982	British Airways	1987
British Leyland (Rover)	1984	British Steel	1989
British Telecom (BT)	1984	Water authorities	1989
British Shipbuilders	1985	Electricity distribution (area boards)	1990
National Bus Company	1985	Electricity generation (PowerGen & National Power)	1991
British Gas	1986	British Coal	1994/5

The case for privatisation

Specific arguments which have been used to justify the privatisation programme include:

- **revenue raising –** Privatisation, or the sale of state-owned assets, provides the government with a short-term source of revenue, which in some years has reached £3–4 billion;
- **reducing public spending and the PSBR –** Since 1979, the Conservative Government has aimed to reduce public spending and the Public Sector Borrowing Requirement (PSBR);
- **the promotion of competition –** Privatisation has been justified on the grounds that it promotes competition through the break-up of monopoly;
- **the promotion of efficiency –** For 'free-market' economists, this is perhaps the most important justification of privatisation. Supporters of privatisation believe that public ownership gives rise to special forms of inefficiency which disappear once an industry moves into the private sector – even if the industry remains a monopoly. They argue that the 'culture' of public ownership makes nationalised industries resistant to change, and that state-owned industries tend to be run in the interest of a 'feather-bedded' workforce protected from market or commercial discipline. By exposing the industry to the threat of takeover and the discipline of the capital market, the privatisation of a state-owned monopoly should improve efficiency and commercial performance;
- **'popular capitalism' –** Undoubtedly an important reason for the privatisation programme in the UK has been the motive of promoting an **'enterprise culture'** through **extending share ownership** to individuals and employees who previously did not own shares, so as to widen the stake of the electorate in supporting a private enterprise economy.

The case against privatisation

- **monopoly abuse –** Opponents of privatisation argue that far from promoting competition and efficiency, privatisation increases monopoly abuse by transferring socially-owned and accountable public monopolies into weakly-regulated and less-accountable private monopolies;
- **short-termism versus long-termism –** Many of the investments which need to be undertaken by the previously-nationalised industries can only be profitable in the long term. There is a danger that, under private ownership, such investments will not be made because company boards concentrate on the 'short-termism' of delivering dividends to keep shareholders and financial institutions happy. Also, nationalised industries can better take account of external costs and benefits;

REVISION SUMMARY

- **'selling the family silver'** – Opponents of privatisation also argue that if a private sector business were to sell its capital assets simply in order to raise revenue to pay for current expenditure, it would rightly incur the wrath of its shareholders. The same should be true of the government and the sale of state-owned assets: taxpayers ought not to sanction the sale of capital assets owned on their behalf by the UK government to raise revenue to finance current spending on items such as wages and salaries;
- **the 'free lunch' syndrome** – Opponents of privatisation also claim that state-owned assets have been sold too cheaply, encouraging the belief amongst first-time share buyers that there is such a thing as a 'free lunch'.

Privatisation and the wider policy of economic liberalisation

So far privatisation has been defined in a strictly narrow sense, as the transfer of assets from the public sector to the private sector. Some commentators extend the definition of privatisation to include other aspects of the programme of **economic liberalisation** pursued by the Conservative Government since 1979. Other policies which are closely related to privatisation are **contractualisation**, **marketisation** and **deregulation**. 'Contractualisation' or **'contracting-out'** takes place when services such as road cleaning and refuse collection are put out to private sector tender, though the taxpayer still ultimately pays for the service. To try to get value for money for the taxpayer, services which were previously provided 'in house' by public sector workers are now put out to **competitive tendering**. Whereas privatisation (narrowly defined) involves transferring assets from the public sector to the private sector, marketisation or **commercialisation** shifts the provision of services from the non-market sector into the market sector by charging a price for a service which consumers previously enjoyed 'free'. An example of this is the **internal market** which has been created within the NHS, where community doctors (GPs) 'shop around' to purchase the best value surgical services on offer from 'providers', i.e. NHS hospitals.

Regulation

'Economic regulation' involves the imposition of rules, controls and constraints which restrict freedom of economic action in the market place. There are two types of regulation: **'external regulation'** which, as the name suggests, involves an external agency laying down and enforcing rules and restraints, and **'self-regulation'** or voluntary regulation. In the case of external regulation, the regulatory agency may be a government department such as the Department of Trade and Industry (DTI), or a body or agency set up by government, for example the **Monopolies and Mergers Commission (MMC)** or the **Office of Fair Trading (OFT)**.

Deregulation

'Deregulation' is literally the opposite of regulation, namely the removal of any previously imposed regulations. There are two main justifications for deregulation: (i) to promote competition and market contestability through the removal of artificial barriers to market entry; and (ii) to remove 'red tape' and bureaucracy which imposes unnecessary costs on economic agents, particularly businesses.

If you need to revise this subject more thoroughly, see the relevant topics in the Letts *A level Economics Study Guide*.

The regulation of the privatised utility industries

But during the same years in which deregulation became a principal instrument in the policy of economic liberalisation, the Conservative Government also privatised the so-called **'natural' monopoly** or **'utility' industries**: telecommunications, gas, water and electricity. The Government realised that once privatised, there was an obvious danger that these industries might abuse their monopoly position and exploit the consumer. For this reason special regulatory bodies, each specific to a particular industry, were set up at the time of privatisation to act as 'watchdogs' over the performance of the utilities in the private sector. These regulatory bodies are the Office of Telecommunications (OFTEL), the Office of Gas Supply (OFGAS), the Office of Water Services (OFWAT) and the Office of Electricity Regulation (OFFER). The establishment of OFTEL, OFGAS, OFWAT and OFFER represents what can be called the **'reregulation'** of the privatised utility industries.

QUESTIONS

1 (a) Why did the government create regulatory agencies such as OFTEL (for the telecommunications industry) and OFGAS (for the gas industry), when it privatised previously nationalised industries? (13)

(b) Discuss the various ways in which such regulatory agencies can influence the performance of these industries. (12)

AEB

2 Argue the case **for** competition between firms generating electricity and **against** competition between firms distributing electricity. (100)

UCLES

3 Read the following passage carefully and answer the questions which follow.

> 'Privatisation is a key element of the Government's economic strategy . . . Our main objective is to promote competition and increase efficiency.'
>
> (John Moore, Financial Secretary to the Treasury, 1983)
>
> Privatisation has been central to the supply-side strategy pursued by the post-1979 Conservative Governments. Ironically, however, the Government did not take over in 1979 with the idea of privatising more than a handful of state-run companies. Initially, it believed that public hostility to the idea of 'selling off the family silver' and creating private monopolies out of nationalised industries would limit the scope for privatisation to a small number of enterprises (e.g. the National Freight Corporation). In the event, the early privatisations proved surprisingly popular, encouraging the Government to raise its sights until eventually giant corporations like British Telecom, British Gas and the electricity industries were sold off.
>
> Compared with their nationalised counterparts, private monopolies typically restrict output and make larger profits, thereby reducing the social benefit. Although the Government has sought to reduce monopoly power, many of the enterprises that have been privatised are natural monopolists, in which the creation of effective competition is very difficult to obtain. Moreover, in the case of natural monopolies, like electricity and gas, not only does the transfer of ownership risk consumer exploitation, but it may also result in the industries becoming less, rather than more, efficient.
>
> Adapted from *A Summary of the UK Economy 1992/93*, D C McCarthy

(a) Explain the meaning of the following terms, as used in the passage:

(i) supply-side strategy; (2)

(ii) social benefit. (2)

(b) For what economic reasons might there be 'public hostility' to the proposed privatisation of nationalised industries? (3)

(c) (i) Explain what is meant by the term 'natural monopoly'. (2)

(ii) Why would governments find it difficult to achieve effective competition when privatising a natural monopoly? (3)

(d) What economic benefits would governments hope to obtain by pursuing privatisation policies? (4)

(e) Privatisation is one method by which governments can introduce more competition into public services. Describe fully other government measures which could achieve this aim.

(4)

SEB

6 *Market failure*

REVISION SUMMARY

Market failure

Market failure occurs whenever the market mechanism or price mechanism performs unsatisfactorily. Market failure can occur for two main reasons: **inequity** and **inefficiency**. In the former case, for example, the distributions of income and wealth brought about through the interplay of unregulated market forces may be deemed too unequal and unfair, and government policies of progressive taxation and transfers to lower income groups may be justified as methods of correcting the market failure. However, the three examples of market failure covered in this unit result primarily from the *inefficient* functioning of the market, although the outcome arising from free market forces might also be regarded as inequitable. These examples are **public goods, externalities**, and **merit** and **demerit goods**.

Public goods

Public goods are an example of market failure resulting from 'missing markets'; in a market economy markets may fail to provide any quantity at all of a **pure public good** such as national defence. A public good is defined by the two characteristics it possesses: **non-excludability** and **non-diminishability**. It is these which lead to market failure. Non-excludability means that if a public good were to be provided through the market with a price being charged to consumers, it would be impossible to exclude **free-riders** – people who consume or benefit without paying. Therefore, the incentive for entrepreneurs to provide the public good breaks down. But most public goods are **non-pure public goods** or **quasi-public goods** rather than pure public goods, because various methods could be devised to exclude free-riders. Non-pure public goods include roads, TV and radio broadcasts, streetlighting and lighthouses. For these goods, their **non-diminishability** creates a strong case for non-market provision. Non-diminishability (or **non-rivalry**) means that whenever an extra individual consumes the benefits of the public good, the benefits available to other consumers are not diminished. It also means that the marginal cost incurred by the provider of the public good when an extra person consumes its benefits is zero. Now, the allocatively efficient or 'correct' quantity of any good occurs when P = MC. It follows, therefore, that to promote allocative efficiency, public goods must be provided at zero price so as to maximise their consumption. But assuming free-riders are excluded, private entrepreneurs are only prepared to provide goods if they can make a profit, which requires a price above zero. Market provision of public goods requires therefore, that P > MC, which, as we have seen, results in their under-production and under-consumption. There is thus a case, even when the goods can be provided through the market, for the state to provide public goods 'free' to the consumer.

Externalities

An **externality** is a special type of public good, or public 'bad', which is 'dumped' by those who produce it on other people (known as 'third parties') who receive or consume it, whether or not they choose to. The key feature of an externality is that there is no market in which it can be bought or sold – externalities are produced and received outside the market. As with public goods, externalities provide examples of the free-rider problem. The provider of an **external benefit** (or **positive externality**) such as a beautiful view cannot charge a market price to any 'willing free-riders' who enjoy it, while conversely, the 'unwilling free-riders' who receive or consume **external costs** (or **negative externalities**), such as pollution and noise, cannot charge a price to the polluter for the 'bad' they reluctantly consume.

Pollution as a negative externality

Consider a power station which discharges pollution into the atmosphere in the course of producing electricity. We can view a negative production externality such as pollution as being that part of the *true* or *real* costs of production which the firm evades by dumping the 'bad' on others. The price the consumer pays for the good (electricity), reflects only the *money* costs of production, and not the external costs. In a market situation, the power station's output of electricity is thus

underpriced, encouraging too much consumption, and therefore also too much production of both electricity and pollution.

Private and social marginal cost and benefit
Because of the negative externality, the **marginal social cost (MSC)** of production to the whole community exceeds the **marginal private cost (MPC)** incurred by the power station. As a result, **private benefit maximisation**, where **marginal private benefit = marginal private cost (MPB = MPC)**, no longer coincides with **social benefit maximisation**, where **marginal social benefit = marginal social cost (MSB = MSC)**. Due to the externality, the MSC > MPC. If the power station maximises its private benefit by producing where MPB = MPC, overproduction of electricity (and of the externality, pollution) occurs. This is shown in the diagram below.

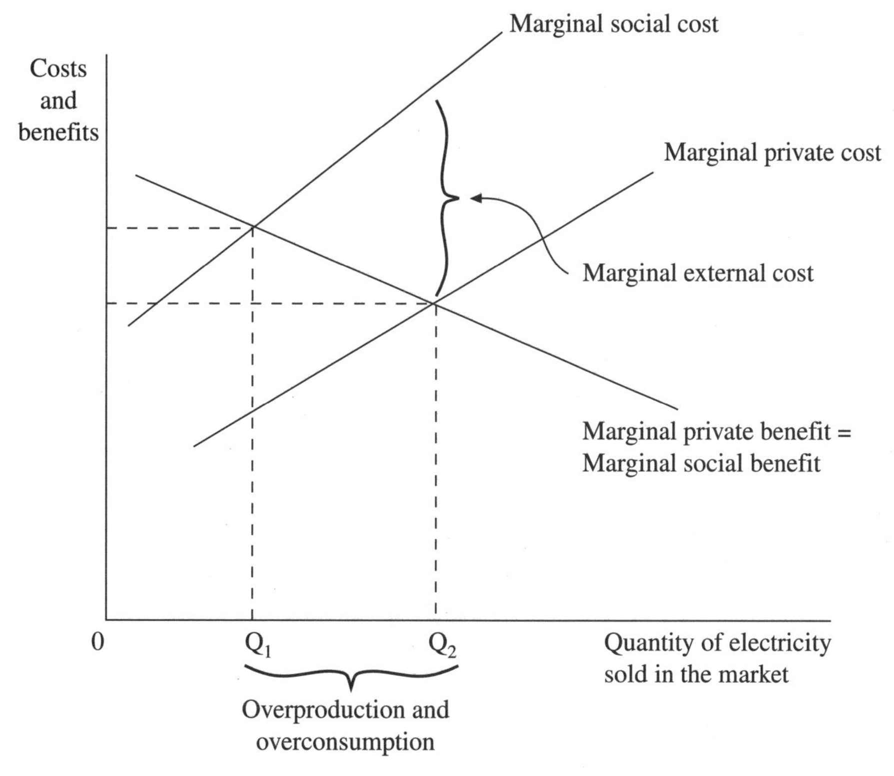

Private and social costs when a negative production externality such as pollution is discharged. Without government intervention, overproduction of both the good (electricity) and the negative externality (pollution) occurs.

Now, allocative efficiency occurs when price equals marginal cost (P = MC). But the price must equal the true marginal cost of production, i.e. the marginal social cost and not just the marginal private cost. However, in a market situation, firms can only take account of private costs and benefits, so when externalities exist, the market mechanism cannot ensure an allocatively efficient equilibrium. Even if the power station company sets the price of electricity where P = MPC, it turns out that P < MSC because the price charged does not reflect the cost of the pollution dumped on others. As a result, too much electricity is sold at too low a price, and too much of the 'bad' – pollution – is also produced.

Public policy and externalities
When externalities are generated in production, the **public policy problem** is to ensure the 'correct' or socially-optimal level of production and consumption of the good which a firm is producing. This occurs at the level of output where MSB = MSC. The two main methods of closing the divergency between private and social cost and benefit and correcting the market failure are **quantity controls** (or **regulation**) and **taxation** or **subsidy**.

Merit goods and demerit goods

Merit goods (and **demerit goods**) provide further examples of divergency between private and social cost and benefit, and of the generation of externalities. A merit good such as education or health care is a good or service from which the social benefits of consumption to the whole community exceed the private benefits to the consumer. Whereas markets may very well fail to provide any quantity at all of a pure public good such as defence, they can certainly provide education and health care, as the existence of private fee-paying schools and hospitals clearly demonstrates. But if schools and hospitals are available only through the market at prices unadjusted by subsidy, people (especially the poor) will choose to consume too little of their services. As their name suggests, demerit goods are the opposite of merit goods. The social costs to the whole community which result from the consumption of a demerit good such as tobacco or alcohol exceed the private costs incurred by the consumer. As with externalities, regulation and taxation or subsidy can be used to try to ensure the socially optimal level of production and consumption of a merit or demerit good.

If you need to revise this subject more thoroughly, see the relevant topics in the *Letts A level Economics Study Guide.*

QUESTIONS

1 (a) 'If a government supplies genuine public goods to individuals, there is no problem of rationing. If, however, a government supplies private goods then often there is a rationing problem involved.' Explain these statements. (15)

(b) Consider how rationing problems are solved:

(i) In the allocation of student places on certain university degree courses. (5)

(ii) In the allocation of NHS hospital services. (5)

WJEC

2 Discuss the economic effects of governments attempting to influence the distribution of real income through the system of taxes and benefits. (20)

Oxford

3 The following passage describes a scheme recently introduced in the USA which aims to reduce the pollution caused by coal-burning power stations. The scheme is based on setting, and then each year gradually reducing, maximum limits or ceilings on pollution. Under the scheme, a power station which 'over-complies', i.e. one which cuts pollution by more than is required, is allowed to sell its spare pollution allowances. The allowance or 'permit to pollute' can be bought by an 'under-complying' power station, i.e. one which has cut pollution by less than is required.

Read the passage and answer the questions that follow:

A Market in 'Permits to Pollute'

Last month, three US utility companies bravely waded into a national experiment to use market principles for environmental ends and to tackle a problem of 'market failure'. In the first public deal to trade 'permits to pollute', the Wisconsin Power & Light Company sold 10,000 allowances to the Tennessee Valley Authority and 15,000–25,000 allowances to Duquesne Light Company in Pittsburgh. 5

The allowances are part of the Clean Air Act of 1990, which requires America's mostly coal-burning utilities to halve their emissions of sulphur dioxide, the key ingredient in acid rain, by the year 2000. The national cap on sulphur dioxide emissions will be achieved in the most economically efficient way by trading the rights to pollute among utilities. Under the Act, those companies which exceed 10 compliance with the emissions standard – by installing new cleaner technology or switching to lower sulphur fuels – can sell their spare allowances, issued by the Environmental Protection Agency (EPA), to those who have not fully complied.

The electricity market is a 'regulatory-driven market'. As yet, however, the public
15 utility commissions that regulate the American power companies have not spelled out who – the consumers of electricity or the companies' shareholders – are to benefit (or lose) from the effects on electricity prices and company costs of the trading of pollution allowances.

At present, surveys show that utility companies are tending towards over-
20 compliance with the new standards, mostly by installing new technology to remove sulphur dioxide from flue gas, and some through fuel switching. The inclination to over-comply means that there will be extra allowances for sale. The price of allowances or 'permits to pollute' should therefore be kept pretty low.

In Phase 1, which runs from 1995 to the year 2000, 110 of the dirtiest plants have
25 been targeted to reduce their emissions. Because most of these power stations are likely to install new technology to reduce emissions in preference to buying extra pollution allowances, the price of pollution permits will probably continue to remain low throughout Phase 1. But after the year 2000, in Phase 2, a permanent annual cap of 8.9m tonnes of sulphur dioxide will be applied to all the electricity generators.
30 Assuming that demand for electricity increases, many power stations will find they are unable to meet demand, while keeping within the pollution ceiling, solely by installing clean technology. To meet the demand for power, they will have to purchase extra pollution allowances. In Phase 2 allowance prices are expected to rise to about $600 per tonne (one allowance equals one tonne of sulphur dioxide). This
35 compares with $250–$300 per tonne in the first deal. The EPA's penalty for emitting excess sulphur dioxide is $2,000 per tonne.

Adapted from: 'A market made out of muck', by Barbara Durr, *Financial Times*, June 10th 1992

(a) Explain briefly why economists regard the formation of acid rain as a 'market failure'. (4)

(b) Explain
   (i) the statement that the electricity market is a 'regulatory-driven market' (line 14); (3)
   (ii) how consumers might benefit from the trading of allowances to pollute (lines 16–18). (3)

(c) With the aid of supply and demand analysis, explain why, according to the passage, the price of pollution permits or allowances is likely to rise from $250–$300 per allowance in Phase 1 to about $600 in Phase 2 (lines 33–34). (6)

(d) The passage states that: 'The national cap on sulphur dioxide emissions will be achieved in the most economically efficient way by trading the rights to pollute . . .' (lines 8–10).
   (i) Briefly describe **one** other method, besides the creation of a market in pollution permits, by which sulphur dioxide pollution might be limited. (2)
   (ii) Discuss the advantages and disadvantages of the various methods of controlling sulphur dioxide pollution. (7)

AEB

7 The labour market and employment issues

REVISION SUMMARY

The supply curve of labour

Assuming a perfectly competitive labour market, the **market supply curve** of labour available to all the employers in the market is obtained simply by *adding* together the **individual supply curves** of all the workers in the particular labour market. An **individual worker's supply curve of labour** shows how many labour hours he or she is prepared to supply at different hourly wage-rates. To maximise utility, a worker must supply labour up to the point at which:

MU of the wage = MU of leisure

When the MU of the wage equals the MU of leisure, a worker is in equilibrium in the sense that there is no further incentive to supply more hours of labour time at the going hourly wage rate. Only if the hourly wage rate rises, will the worker supply more labour. Hence the upward-sloping supply curve of labour shown in the left-hand panel of the diagram below:

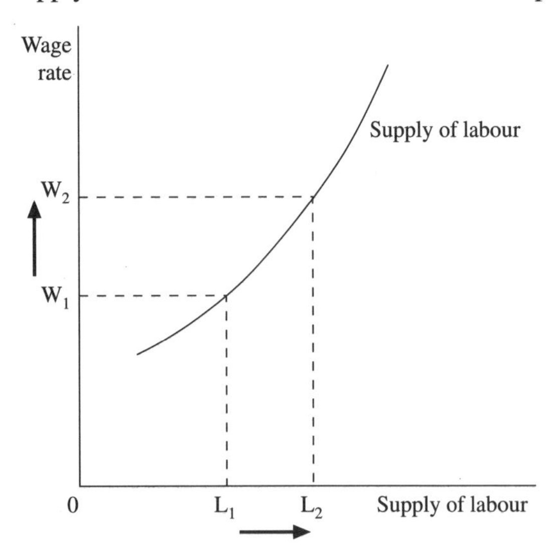

The upward-sloping supply curve of labour

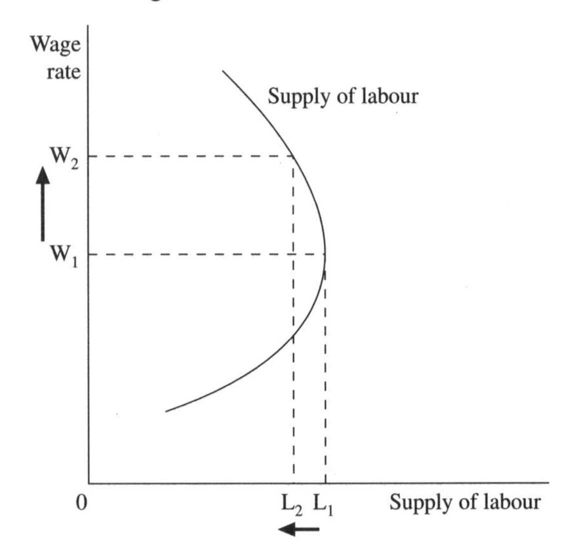

The backward-bending supply curve of labour

The backward-bending supply curve of labour

Under some circumstances, however, a worker's labour supply curve may be **'backward-bending'**, showing that as the wage rises, less labour is supplied. This is illustrated in the right-hand panel of the diagram, where the supply curve has been drawn 'upward-sloping' for only part of its length. According to the **substitution effect** of a wage rate change, a worker's supply curve should slope upwards, showing the individual substituting 'labour time' for 'leisure time' as the hourly wage rate increases. However, matters are complicated by the **income effect** resulting from a wage rate change. The income effect of a wage rate increase results from the fact that for most people 'leisure time' is a **normal good** and *not* an inferior good. A rise in the hourly wage rate increases the worker's real income, and as real income rises, so does the demand for the 'normal' good, leisure. Up to the wage rate W_1 in the right-hand panel of the diagram, the substitution effect of any wage increase exceeds the income effect and the worker chooses more work and less leisure. But beyond the wage rate W_1, the income effect of a wage rise becomes more powerful than the substitution effect. As a result, the worker chooses to work fewer hours so as to enjoy more leisure, hence the backward-bending supply curve of labour!

The demand curve for labour

Just as the market supply curve of labour in a perfectly competitive labour market is the sum of the supply curves of all the individual workers in the labour market, so the market demand curve for labour is obtained by adding together each firm's demand curve for labour at different wage rates. A firm's demand for labour – or indeed its demand for the services of any factor of production – is a **derived demand**. The services of labour are demanded not for any utility directly yielded to the

firm, but only because they are necessary as inputs to produce outputs of goods and services for sale at a profit in the goods market. Assuming a profit-maximising objective on the part of firms, there can be no demand for factor services in the long run unless the firms sell the outputs produced for at least a normal profit in the goods market.

In a perfectly competitive labour market, a firm's demand curve for labour is the **marginal revenue product (MRP)** of labour curve which faces the firm. At any level of employment, the MRP curve is derived from the following relationship:

$$\text{Marginal Physical Product} \times \text{Marginal Revenue} \equiv \text{Marginal Revenue Product}$$

or:

$$MPP \times MR \equiv MRP$$

The law of diminishing returns explains the negative slope of the MPP curve drawn in the left-hand panel of the diagram below, which shows the marginal product of labour falling as additional workers are hired by the firm. The MRP curve of labour shown in the right-hand panel of the diagram, is thus obtained by multiplying the MPP of labour by the horizontal MR curve drawn in the middle panel.

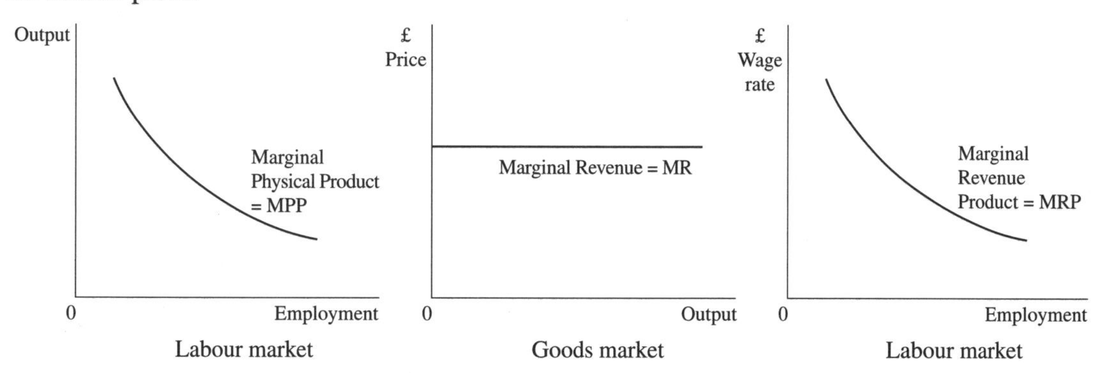

Labour market equilibrium

We are now in a position to show the determination of both the **equilibrium wage** and **level of employment** in the *whole labour market*, and also the determination of equilibrium employment or demand for labour at the level of a *single firm* within the market. These are shown in the next diagram.

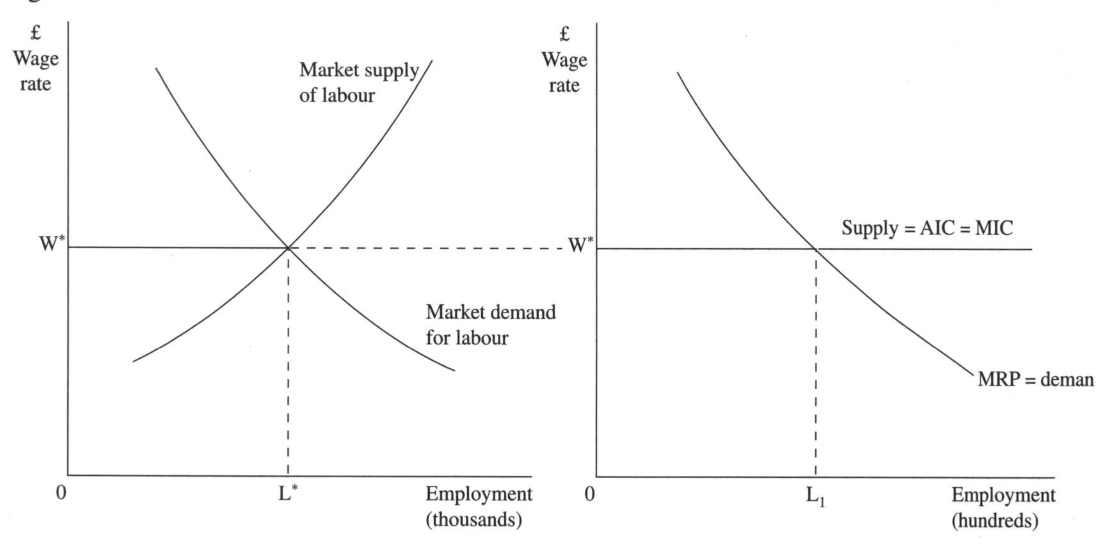

REVISION SUMMARY

The equilibrium wage and equilibrium employment for the *whole labour market* are shown in the left-hand panel of the diagram on page 27, at the intersection of the market demand curve for labour and the market supply curve of labour. The right-hand panel shows how the ruling market wage W* affects individual firms within the market. Each firm is a **price-taker at the ruling wage**, which is both the **perfectly elastic supply curve of labour** facing the firm and the **average** and **marginal input cost curve (AIC** and **MIC)**. A firm can therefore employ as much labour as it wishes at the ruling market wage, but *it cannot influence the ruling wage by its own actions*. In order to maximise profits when it eventually sells the output produced by labour, the firm *must* choose the level of employment at which:

$$MRP = MIC$$

And since in a perfectly competitive labour market, the marginal input cost incurred by the firm always equals the actual wage paid to the workers, we can write the equilibrium equation as:

$$MRP = W$$

The causes of unemployment

In a perfectly competitive labour market there should be no unemployment, provided that the market mechanism operates smoothly and the labour market clears. However, if the market mechanism fails to function efficiently, unemployment may be caused by the wage rate remaining too high to clear the market. The resulting unemployment is known as **classical** or **real wage unemployment**. But even if the labour market clears, there may still be some frictional and structural unemployment. Frictional unemployment, as its name suggests, results from frictions in the labour market which create a delay or time-lag during which a worker is unemployed when moving from one job to another. **Structural unemployment** results from the **structural decline** of industries, unable to compete or adapt in the face of either changing demand and new products, or changing ways of producing existing products and the emergence of more efficient competitors in other countries. **Technological unemployment** can be regarded as a special case of structural unemployment, which results from the successful growth of new industries using labour-saving technology such as **automation**.

The natural rate of unemployment

The more competitive and adaptable the economy is, then the lower will be the level of frictional and structural unemployment caused by the dynamic nature of the economy. Monetarists and free-market supply-side economists call this minimum level of unemployment the **natural rate of unemployment (NRU)**. Some economists restrict the definition of the natural rate to frictional unemployment only, while others extend the definition to include structural unemployment.

If you need to revise this subject more thoroughly, see the relevant topics in the *Letts A level Economics Study Guide*.

Keynesian or demand-deficient unemployment

Keynes believed that **deficient aggregate demand** was a major cause of persistent mass unemployment between the First and Second World Wars in the 1920s and 1930s. Keynes argued that the economy could settle into the **'under-full employment equilibrium'** caused by a continuing lack of effective aggregate demand. Monetarist and supply-side economists believe that in a competitive market economy, market forces quickly eliminate demand deficiency, though temporary demand-deficient unemployment occurs in the downswing of the business cycle.

QUESTIONS

1 What are the main causes of wage differentials in the labour market? Women make up some 47 per cent of the labour market in Britain while female earnings are about 80 per cent of those of men. Does economic theory satisfactorily account for the pattern of employment and pay? (25)
NEAB

2 (a) Explain what is meant by 'the natural rate of unemployment' (also known as NAIRU). (30)

(b) Evaluate the effects of demand-side and supply-side policies on the natural rate of unemployment. (70)
ULEAC

3 Compare Keynesian and 'supply-side' policies for reducing unemployment. (25)
WJEC

8 Macroeconomic policy

REVISION SUMMARY

The distinction between macroeconomics and microeconomics

Whereas **microeconomics** examines the economic behaviour of economic agents such as households and firms in the individual markets that make up the economy, **macroeconomics** examines the functioning of the whole economy. Macroeconomics studies the **aggregates** in the economy – the determinants of the overall levels of output, employment and unemployment, the price level (and its rate of change, the inflation rate), and the trade flows which make up the balance of payments.

The objectives of macroeconomic policy

Macroeconomic policy comprises the government economic policies which aim to improve the economic performance of the whole economy. It is usual to identify five principal objectives of government macroeconomic policy. These are:

- full employment;
- economic growth (and higher living standards and levels of economic welfare);
- a fair or equitable distribution of income and wealth;
- control of inflation;
- a satisfactory balance of payments.

Keynesian macroeconomics

The order in which we have just listed the objectives of macroeconomic policy is not accidental. It represents a **Keynesian** ranking or ordering of priority of the objectives of macroeconomic policy. During the **Keynesian era** (which lasted from the 1940s to the 1970s), British governments implemented Keynesian macroeconomic policies aimed at achieving full employment, economic growth and a more equal or equitable distribution of income and wealth, namely the objectives we have placed at the head of the list. During the Keynesian era, macroeconomic policy was used primarily to manage the level of aggregate demand to try to achieve relatively full employment and economic growth, without excessive inflation or an unsustainable deterioration in the balance of payments.

Policy trade-offs

In order to achieve full employment and economic growth, Keynesian governments **reflated** the economy by injecting demand into the economy. **Monetary policy** and **fiscal policy** (which are explained in Unit 11) were used for this purpose. By cutting interest rates (as a part of monetary policy) and taxes (fiscal policy), the government expanded the economy, stimulating output and employment. But Keynesian policy makers found that whenever they expanded demand to increase growth and reduce unemployment, the balance of payments deteriorated and/or inflation began to accelerate. In effect, the government's freedom to pursue the macroeconomic policy of its choice was constrained by the existence of policy trade-offs.

Over the years, UK macro-policy has been influenced and constrained by three significant policy trade-offs. These have been:

- The trade-off between the **'internal' policy objectives** of full employment and growth and the **'external' objective** of achieving a satisfactory balance of payments (and possibly supporting a particular exchange rate);
- The trade-off between **full employment** and **control of inflation**, often called the Phillips curve trade-off;
- The trade-off between **economic growth** and a **more equal distribution of income and wealth**.

REVISION SUMMARY

Monetarism

Towards the end of the Keynesian era in the 1970s, there was a simultaneous failure in the UK to achieve any of the primary policy objectives. The **'stagflation'** or **'slumpflation'** of stagnant or declining output and growing unemployment combined with accelerating inflation, together with social conflict over the distribution of income and a deteriorating balance of payments, brought the Keynesian era to an end. Since then, economic policy – micro as well as macro – has been strongly influenced by monetarism and 'supply-side' economics. Narrowly defined, **monetarism** centres on the proposition that the immediate cause of all inflation lies in a prior increase, permitted by governments, of the money supply. More loosely defined, monetarism is the economics of a self-adjusting or self-regulating private enterprise market economy subject to minimal government intervention and regulation. The **quantity theory of money** underpins monetarist macroeconomic policy. According to the quantity theory, if the government allows the money supply to expand at a rate faster than the growth of output, the price level rises when people spend the excess money balances which they hold.

Supply-side economics

During the early 1980s, UK macroeconomic policy could be described as monetarist. The Government used monetary policy (backed up by fiscal policy) to try to hit preannounced money supply targets, in the belief that such 'monetary targetry' was necessary in order to control inflation. However, the policy was difficult to operate and was not very effective, an outcome which had an adverse effect on the credibility deemed necessary for the policy to be able to work. After about 1986, the strictly monetarist aspects of macro-economic policy were quietly dropped by the Conservative Government, though it remained committed to controlling inflation as the primary objective of macroeconomic policy, and to the wider free-market aspects of its economic policy. The term 'supply-side economics' is now used to describe the theories upon which recent economic policy has been based. As with monetarism, supply-side economics has both a narrow and a broad meaning. Narrowly interpreted, supply-side economics centres on fiscal policy and tax cuts and their effects on incentives to supply labour, to be entrepreneurial and to save. More broadly, we can define supply-side economic policy as the set of government economic policies which aims to change the underlying structure of the economy and improve both the economic performance of markets and industries, and also that of individual firms and workers within markets. It is worth noting that many supply-side policies are microeconomic rather than macroeconomic.

If you need to revise this subject more thoroughly, see the relevant topics in the *Letts A level Economics Study Guide*.

QUESTIONS

1 'UK governments have difficulty in achieving all their economic objectives simultaneously.'

(a) Describe briefly the main economic objectives of recent UK governments. (6)

(b) Give a full account of the main measures that can be used to achieve these objectives. (14)

(c) Why is it difficult for governments to achieve these objectives simultaneously? (10)

SEB

2 'Inflation is triggered by excess demand but sustained by rising costs.'

(a) Explain this statement. (15)

(b) Discuss its implications for the successful control of inflation. (10)

AEB

QUESTIONS

3 Read the article below on the Retail Price Index and then answer the questions that follow.

The cost of living as measured by the RPI

The Retail Price Index has been criticised in a recent report from the Institute of Fiscal Studies because whilst it generally overstates price rises, it also underplays their effect on the poor.

The RPI is very important to the government because it determines the value of state pensions and social security benefits as well as personal tax allowances and index-linked national savings. All of these and other components of government spending are automatically increased in line with rises in the RPI.

The report concludes that for many years the RPI has exaggerated the rate of inflation and thus government spending has been unnecessarily high. One explanation for this phenomenon is that the weights used in the calculations of the RPI reflect the quantities of goods and services bought in the year preceding the newly calculated index. As a result the index does not accurately reflect current spending habits, so that if the price of one product increases and people purchase a substitute at a lower price, it may be up to two years before the new data is reflected in the index. For this reason the inflation rate is overestimated.

Another criticism of the RPI made by the IFS is that it disregards improvements in the quality of goods. 'Price increases are not fully inflationary if higher prices reflect improved quality.'

Whilst in general terms the RPI overstates the rate of inflation, for low income earners the RPI may understate their 'personal inflation rates'. If, for example, the prices of goods which are heavily purchased by the poor go up disproportionately, such as coal and electricity, the poor will be faced by higher prices than the rich. The IFS calculates between 1974 and 1982 the bottom 10 per cent of households faced price increases on average 8 per cent above those that the richest 10 per cent faced.

Benefits which are indexed linked to the RPI and earmarked for the poor will in fact incur a reduction in their real value.

Items included in the Retail Price Index

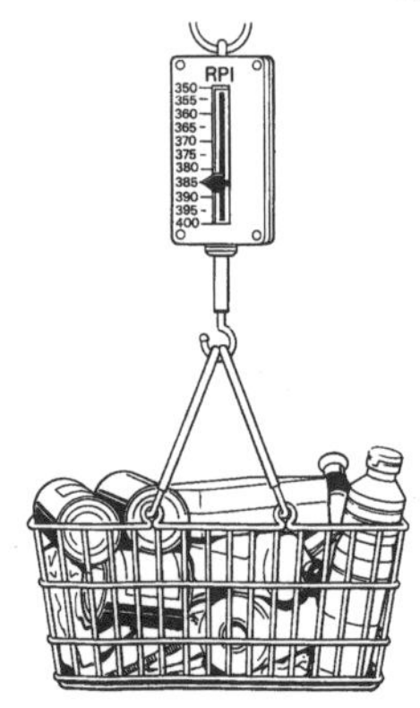

	Weights, 1984
Food	201
Alcoholic drink	75
Tobacco	36
Housing	149
Fuel and light	65
Durable household goods	69
Clothing and footwear	70
Transport and vehicles	158
Miscellaneous goods	76
Services	65
Meals bought and consumed outside the home	36
Total	1000

Source: Monthly Digest of Statistics, CSO

(a) Explain briefly how the RPI is constructed and give two problems related to its construction. (4)

(b) (i) Why is the RPI 'very important to government'?
(ii) What other uses can be made of the RPI? (5)

(c) Why did the Institute of Fiscal Studies Report suggest that the RPI overstates the increase in the cost of living? (5)

(d) Why might the RPI not be an accurate measure of the change in the cost of living of lower income groups and what are the implications? (6)

Oxford & Cambridge

The meaning of consumption, saving and investment

Great care must be taken in understanding the use made by economists of the terms consumption, saving and investment. In macroeconomic theory, we define **consumption** as the spending by all the households in the economy upon goods and services produced within the economy. Aggregate consumption does *not* include household expenditure upon **imports** which are part of the goods and services produced in other countries. Nor does it include investment. Economists make a clear separation between saving and investment, even though in everyday language the two terms are often used interchangeably. **Saving** is income which is not consumed, but **investment** is expenditure by firms on capital goods.

The propensities to consume and save

The 'propensity to consume' and the 'propensity to save' are terms which economists use to measure planned or intended consumption and saving as a ratio of income. At any level of income (Y), the **average propensity to consume (APC)** measures total planned consumption as a ratio of the level of income. Likewise, the **average propensity to save (APS)** measures total planned saving as a ratio of income. Since it is very easy to confuse the average propensity to consume or APC with the **marginal propensity to consume (MPC)**, make sure that you learn the distinction between the two concepts. The MPC measures a change in planned consumption as a ratio of change in the level of income. In a similar way, the **marginal propensity to save (MPS)** measures the change in planned saving as a ratio of a change in income.

The personal saving ratio

The propensities to consume and save indicate how much people *wish* or *plan* to consume and to save at different levels of income rather than how much they *actually end up* consuming and saving. Because of the difficulty of measurement, the **personal saving ratio**, which is often used as an approximate indicator of the average propensity to save, measures the **actual** or **realised** savings of the personal sector as a ratio of total personal sector disposal income.

The determinants of consumption and saving

A large number of factors determine the aggregate levels of consumption and saving in the economy. According to the **Keynesian theory of consumption** illustrated in the following diagram, the level of income is the main determinant of consumption. Aggregate planned consumption rises as income rises, but at a slower rate than income. As household income grows, the proportion of income consumed falls, while the proportion saved rises.

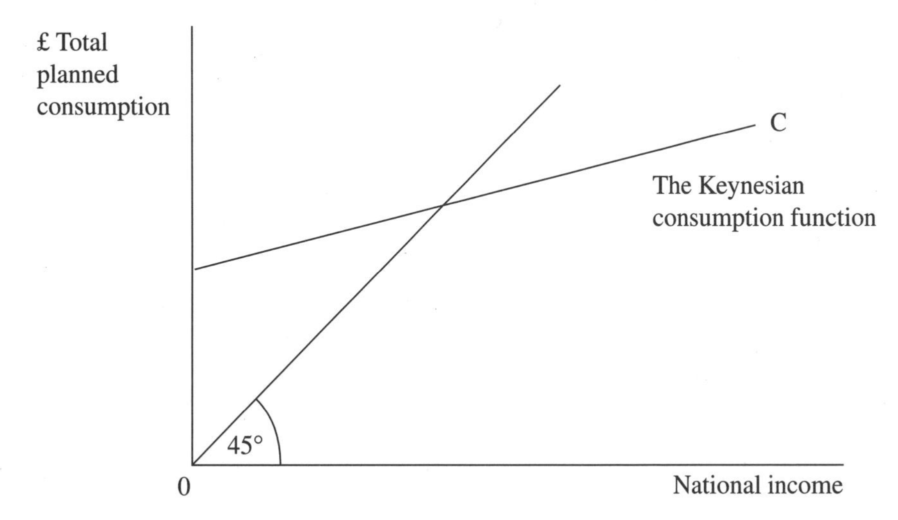

According to the **'life-cycle'** and **'permanent income' theories of consumption**, consumption and savings decisions are determined not just by current income, but by income households expect

REVISION SUMMARY

to receive in the future. Other influences upon consumption and saving decisions include wealth, the rate of interest, and the availability of credit.

The marginal efficiency of capital

The **marginal efficiency of capital (MEC)** theory is the first of two theories of investment tested in the A-level examination. In the MEC theory, the level of aggregate investment in the economy is determined by two factors, namely the expected future productivity of all the investment projects available for businesses to undertake, and the rate of interest or cost of borrowing. At any point in time, there will be thousands, if not millions, of *potential* investment projects not yet undertaken in the economy, each with its own expected future productivity. If you were to calculate the expected future productivity for every possible capital project available to all the business enterprises in the economy, the investments could be ranked in descending order of expected future yields. Plotted in the following graph, the resulting downward-sloping curve shows the marginal efficiency of capital. With the rate of interest or cost of borrowing at r_1, the equilibrium level of aggregate investment is determined in the diagram below at the point where the marginal efficiency of capital equals the cost of borrowing.

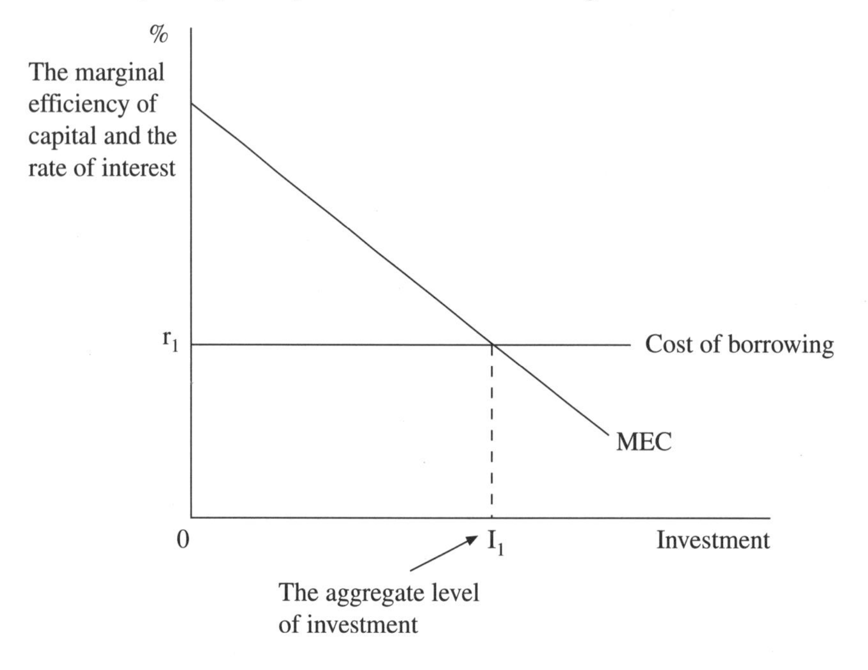

If you need to revise this subject more thoroughly, see the relevant topics in the Letts A level Economics Study Guide.

The accelerator theory

The **accelerator theory** is the second theory of investment you need to know. The theory stems from the rather simple and mechanical assumption that firms wish to keep a relatively fixed ratio, known as the capital–output ratio, between the output they are currently producing and their existing stock of fixed capital assets. If output grows by a *constant* amount each year, firms will invest in exactly the same amount of new capital each year to enlarge their capital stock so as to maintain the desired capital–output ratio. The level of investment will therefore be constant. But if the rate of growth of output speeds up or *accelerates*, investment will also increase as firms take action to enlarge the stock of capital to a level sufficient to maintain the desired capital–output ratio. Conversely, if the rate of growth of output slows down or *decelerates*, investment declines.

The investment multiplier

The investment multiplier measures the relationship between a change in investment and the resulting change in the equilibrium level of national income. A multiplier of 3 means that, following an increase in investment of £2 billion, national income would rise by £6 billion.The size of the multiplier depends on the extent to which income leaks into saving, taxation and imports, rather than being spent on consumption, at each stage of the multiplier process.

QUESTIONS

1 Examine the factors that could determine the aggregate level of investment in a country of your choice. (100)
ULEAC

2 Discuss the economic relationships between consumption, income and investment. (25)
AEB

3 *Figure 1: Saving as a percentage of GDP in the UK, 1970–1989*

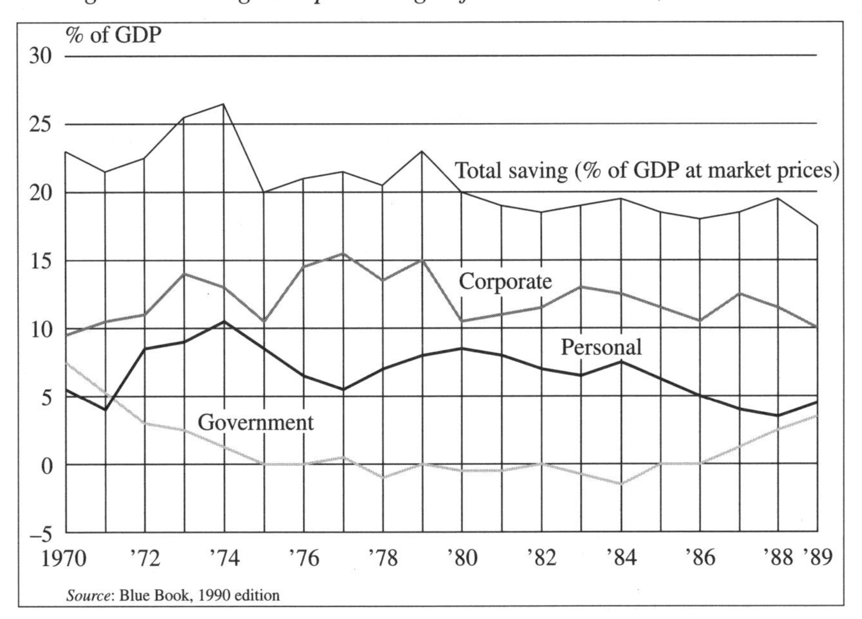

In Figure 1, saving as a percentage of GDP is shown both in total and for each of three sectors of the UK economy.

- The government sector comprises central government and local authorities.
- The personal sector comprises households, unincorporated businesses, life assurance and pension funds, and private non-profit making bodies such as universities.
- The corporate sector comprises industrial and commercial companies, financial companies and institutions, and public corporations.

Figure 2: Personal sector saving ratio in the UK, 1979–1990

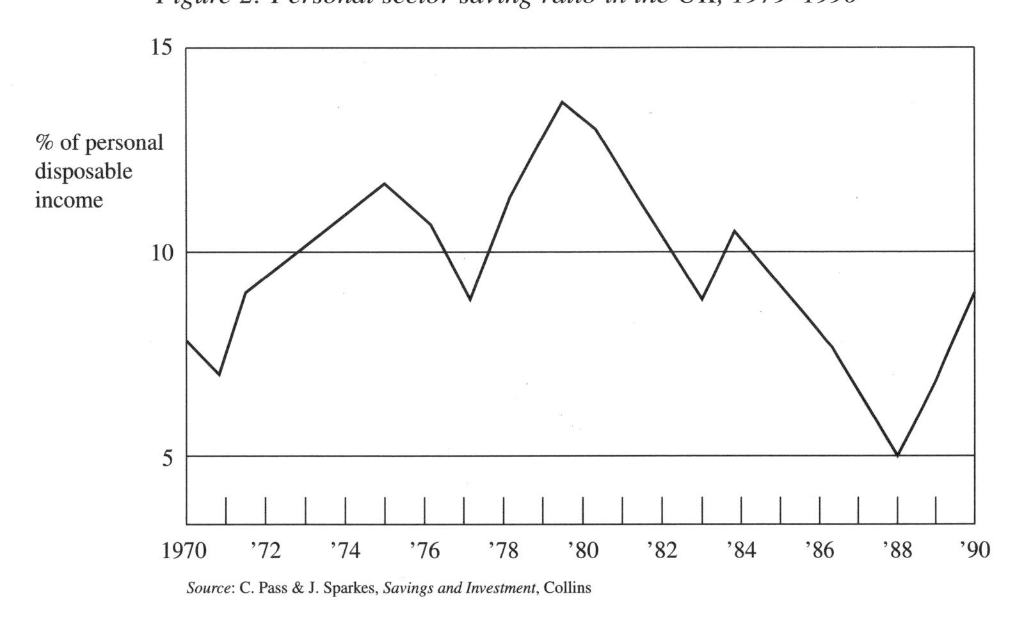

QUESTIONS

Please refer to Figure 1 and Figure 2 on page 35.

(a) Why are the personal saving ratios different in the two diagrams? Explain your answer. (4)

(b) With reference to Figure 1, examine factors likely to explain trends in savings by:

(i) the corporate sector;

(ii) the government sector;

(iii) the personal sector. (3 × 3)

(c) In the decade after 1980, the personal saving ratio fell to an unprecedentedly low level. Discuss the impact you would expect this changing behaviour to have on the level of aggregate demand. (4)

(d) In the period after 1988, the UK economy moved into recession and the personal saving ratio started to rise again. In what way does a rise in the personal saving ratio have an impact on an economy and on the prospects of recovery from recession? (3)

ULEAC

Taxation, government spending and the PSBR 10

REVISION SUMMARY

Taxation and other sources of government revenue

Taxation is the principal source of government revenue for most economies. In the financial year 1994/95, the total receipts from taxation collected by central and local government in the UK amounted to £194 billion, out of a total government revenue of £253bn. Thus taxation accounted for approximately 76 per cent of total revenue, rising to over 93 per cent if **National Insurance contributions** (which were £42.5bn) are included as a form of taxation.

Methods of classifying taxes

A tax, which is a compulsory levy charged by government or by a public authority to pay for its expenditure, can be classified in a number of ways:

- **according to who levies the tax –** In the UK about 90 per cent of total taxation is levied by central government, with local government taxation – at present mostly the council tax – accounting for the remaining 10 per cent of taxation levied by government.
- **according to what is taxed –** The diagram below illustrates the relative importance in the UK in 1994/95 of the three main categories of taxation on income, expenditure and capital, as a proportion of all sources of general government revenue. Taxes on income raised 33 per cent of total revenue, with this figure rising to 50 per cent if National Insurance and other social security contributions are included. Taxes on expenditure raised a further 28 per cent of government revenue, but capital taxes (mostly inheritance tax) are insignificant, raising less than 2 per cent of revenue in the UK;
- **direct and indirect taxation –** These concepts are often used interchangeably with **taxes on income and expenditure**, though it is not strictly true that a tax on spending *must* be an indirect tax. Income tax is a **direct tax** because the person who receives and benefits from the income is liable to pay the tax. By contrast, *most* taxes on spending are **indirect taxes** since the seller of the good, and not the purchaser who benefits from its consumption, is liable to pay the tax. Nevertheless, the purchaser indirectly pays some or all of the tax when the seller passes on the incidence of the tax through a price rise.

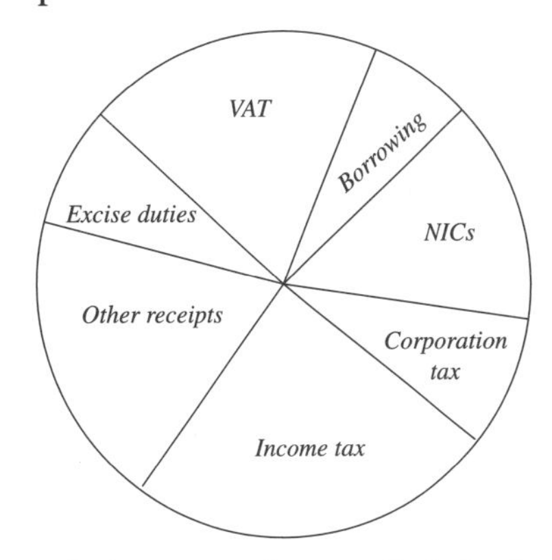

Taxation and other sources of revenue (including borrowing) as properties of total government revenue in the UK, 1995–96

Progressive, proportionate and regressive taxation

In a **progressive tax system**, the proportion of a person's income paid in tax *increases* as income rises, while in a **regressive tax system**, the proportion paid in tax *falls*. **A tax is proportionate** if exactly the same proportion of income is paid in tax at all levels of income. Progressivity can be defined for a single tax or for the tax system as a whole. For single taxes, such as income tax or inheritance tax, we can identify whether the tax is progressive, regressive or proportionate by examining the relationship between the **average rate** at which the tax is levied and the **marginal rate**. For income tax to be progressive, the marginal rate at which the tax is levied must be higher than the average rate, though the average rate which measures the proportion of income paid in tax

REVISION SUMMARY

rises as income increases. Conversely, with a regressive income tax, the marginal rate of tax is less than the average rate, while the two are equal in the case of a proportionate tax. As a general rule, the average tax rate indicates the overall burden of the tax upon the taxpayer, but the marginal rate may significantly affect economic choice and decision-making, in the case of an income tax influencing the choice between work and leisure and decisions on how much labour to supply.

The canons or principles of taxation

Taxpayers commonly view all taxes as 'bad', in the sense that they do not enjoy paying them, though most realise that taxation is necessary in order to provide for the useful goods and services produced by the government. A starting point for analysing and evaluating the 'goodness' or 'badness' of a tax is provided by Adam Smith's four **canons** or **principles** of taxation. Smith suggested that taxation should be **equitable**, **economical**, **convenient** and **certain**, and to these we may add the canons of efficiency and flexibility. A 'good' tax meets as many of these canons as possible, though because of trade-offs it is usually impossible for a tax to meet all of them, while a 'bad' tax meets few, if any, of the guiding principles of taxation.

The aims of taxation and public spending

The aims of both taxation and public spending depend upon the underlying philosophy and ideology of the government in power, differing significantly, for example, between **Keynesianism** on the one hand and free-market **'supply-side' economists** on the other. We may divide the aims or objectives of taxation (and of public spending) into three main categories: **allocation**, **distribution** and **economic management**.

- **Allocation –** The allocative function of taxation and public spending relates largely to the goods and services directly provided to final users by the government, such as public goods and merit goods. Taxes and subsidies may also be used to try to correct the misallocation of resources resulting from other market failures, for example the production of externalities (see Unit 6).
- **Distribution –** If the government were to decide that the distribution of income – and possibly also the distribution of wealth – resulting from free market forces is undesirable, it could use **progressive taxation** and **transfers** to poorer income groups in its public spending programme to modify these distributions and reduce this market failure resulting from inequity.
- **Economic management –** Taxation, public spending and the budget deficit or surplus provide the government with a range of **policy instruments**, known collectively as **fiscal policy instruments**, which the government can use in its overall management of the economy in pursuit of its economic objectives (see Unit 11).

If you need to revise this subject more thoroughly, see the relevant topics in the *Letts A level Economics Study Guide*.

The government's budgetary position

Using the symbols **G** for government spending and **T** for taxation and other sources of revenue, the three possible budgetary positions of the government (and of the whole of the public sector) are:

G = **T** : balanced budget
G > **T** : budget deficit
G < **T** : budget surplus

Budget deficits and the PSBR

A **budget deficit** exists when public sector expenditure exceeds revenue. A budget deficit can be eliminated by cutting public spending or by raising taxation, both of which can balance the budget or move it into surplus. Assuming a deficit persists, it must be financed by borrowing. The borrowing which finances the central government budget deficit is known as the central government borrowing requirement (CGBR). But central government is only one part of the public sector, which also includes local government and nationalised industries. The **public sector borrowing requirement** or **PSBR** is made up of the borrowing of three components: central government; local authorities (which, together with the central government, forms the general government borrowing requirement); and public corporations such as the BBC. The PSBR is thus

REVISION SUMMARY

'the other side of the coin' to the budget deficit. Whenever there is a budget deficit there will be a *positive* borrowing requirement.

Budget surpluses and the PSDR

By contrast, a budget surplus means that the government can use the excess of revenue over expenditure to repay previous borrowing. In this situation, the **public sector debt repayment (PSDR)**, which is associated with a *negative* borrowing requirement, is perhaps a more appropriate measure of the government's net borrowing position than the PSBR.

QUESTIONS

1 In 1978 the standard rate of income tax in the UK was 33% and the top rate was 83%; in 1990 the standard rate was 25% and the top rate was 40%. Examine the likely economic consequences of these changes. (100)
ULEAC

2 Discuss the factors which determine the pattern and level of public expenditure. Illustrate your answer by reference to recent changes in public expenditure. (25)
AEB

3 Study the graph below, then answer the questions which follow:

UK PUBLIC SECTOR FINANCES (1980–1992)

Public Sector Borrowing Requirement (+) Public Sector Debt Repayment (–)

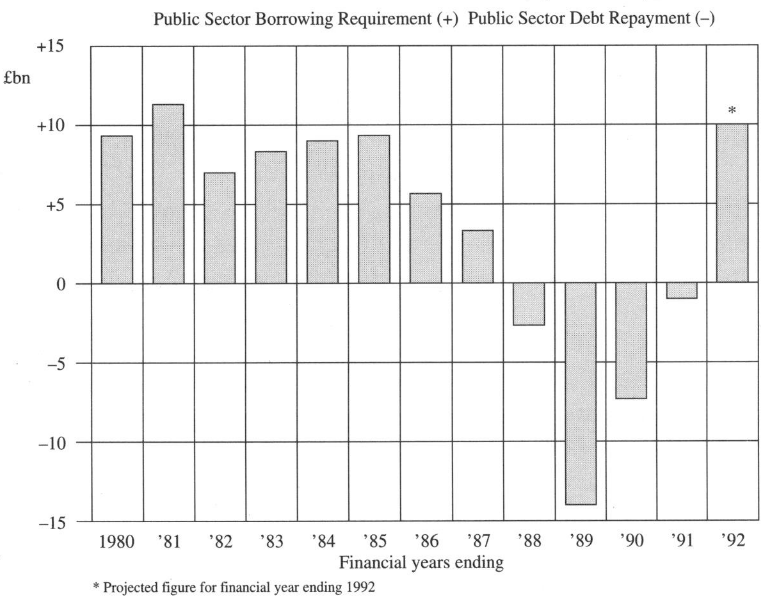

* Projected figure for financial year ending 1992

(a) What do you understand by the terms Public Sector Borrowing Requirement and the Public Sector Debt Repayment? (3)

(b) Give reasons why the UK public sector finances are not always in balance year by year. (3)

(c) The Chancellor of the Exchequer was able to repay debt substantially in 1989, despite cutting direct taxation **and** increasing public sector spending in 1987 and 1988. What changes in the economy made this possible? (4)

(d) (i) How, in theory, do public sector finances react during periods of recession? (3)

(ii) The UK economy has experienced periods of recession which began in 1981 and 1990. Compare the reactions of the public sector finances to these different periods of recession. (3)

(iii) What factors could account for any **differences** or **similarities** you have noted between these reactions? (4)
SEB

11 *Monetary policy and fiscal policy*

REVISION SUMMARY

The meaning of monetary policy

Monetary policy can be defined as any deliberate action undertaken by the government or its agents, such as the country's central bank, to achieve the government's economic objectives using 'monetary instruments', such as controls over bank lending and the rate of interest. Monetary policy is implemented by the country's **monetary authorities**, namely the government's **finance ministry** and the **central bank**. In the UK, these are the **Treasury** and the **Bank of England**.

The instruments of monetary policy

There are a number of policy instruments which the monetary authorities could use to implement monetary policy. These include:

- **'open market operations' –** or the buying or selling of government securities by the Bank of England on the open market (i.e. the capital market and sometimes the money market), in order to influence the banking system's ability to create credit and bank deposits. A sale of government securities (gilts) to the general public, over and above those needed to finance the PSBR, should lead, via the money multiplier, to a multiple contraction of credit and total bank deposits. This is known as **'over-funding' the PSBR**.
- **imposing required reserve ratios upon the banks –** Instead of leaving the clearing banks free to decide their own prudent ratios, the monetary authorities can impose required reserve asset ratios upon the banks. The central bank could then simply raise the required reserve ratio to engineer a contraction of bank deposits.
- **imposing direct controls on the banks –** These could be of two types: **quantitative controls** such as ceilings limiting the amount banks can lend; and **qualitative controls** or **'directional'** controls which instruct, or possibly persuade, banks to lend only to certain types of customers.
- **control via interest rates –** All the techniques of monetary control so far listed operate on the ability of the retail banks to supply credit and to create bank deposits. By contrast, by raising interest rates, the authorities seek to ration demand for credit or bank loans via price.

The instruments and objectives of recent UK monetary policy

For most of the years since 1979, the Bank of England and the Treasury have based monetary policy on the use of a single policy instrument, **interest rates**, to try to achieve a single objective, namely **control of inflation**. Under the influence of free-market, supply-side and monetarist theory, interventionist monetary policy instruments such as required reserve ratios and direct controls have been abandoned on the grounds that they create inefficiencies and make the banking system uncompetitive.

The changing strategy of monetary policy

But while control of inflation has remained the ultimate policy objective, the overall strategy of monetary policy has changed quite significantly since 1979. In the early 1980s, monetary policy was 'monetarist', aiming to achieve price stability by first controlling the rate of growth of the money supply. The authorities operated monetary policy to try to hit a published **money supply target**, which functioned as an **intermediate policy objective**. But between the mid-1980s and 1992, the **exchange rate** replaced the money supply as the intermediate target of monetary policy. Interest rates were set so as to support a high exchange rate, which from 1990 to 1992 was fixed within the exchange rate mechanism (ERM) of the European Monetary System. A high exchange rate was supposed to provide a source of external discipline against inflationary pressures within the UK domestic economy. Finally, since exit from the ERM in 1992, intermediate targets have been dropped and monetary policy has been directed explicitly at a **published inflation rate target**. This is known as **'pre-emptive' monetary policy** – so called because the authorities have announced that they are prepared to raise interest rates even when there is no immediate sign of accelerating inflation, to anticipate and pre-empt a rise in the inflation rate that would otherwise occur many months ahead.

REVISION SUMMARY

The meaning of fiscal policy

Fiscal policy is the part of a government's overall economic policy which aims to achieve the government's economic objectives through the use of the fiscal instruments of taxation, public spending and the budget deficit or surplus. As an economic term, fiscal policy is often associated with **Keynesian** economic theory and policy, largely because Keynes was influential in advocating the abandonment of the 'fiscal orthodoxy' of 'sound finance' and balanced budgets, and the adoption of an active fiscal policy as the most important single instrument of government economic management. In the Keynesian era from the 1950s to the 1970s, fiscal policy came to mean the use of the overall levels of public spending, taxation and the budget deficit to manage the level of aggregate money demand (AMD) in the economy, so as to achieve full employment and stabilise the business cycle. In particular, the budget deficit was used as a fiscal policy instrument for injecting demand into the economy, in the belief that, providing there was unemployment and spare capacity, output and employment would be stimulated without an excessive cost in terms of inflation.

Monetarist and supply-side fiscal policy

It is wrong, however, to associate fiscal policy exclusively with Keynesianism. Since 1979, Keynesian fiscal policy, which was based on the macroeconomic management of aggregate demand, has been superseded by a very different monetarist or supply-side fiscal policy. During the Keynesian era, the overall stance of fiscal policy – and indeed of economic policy in general – was both macroeconomic and orientated towards the demand-side of the economy, under the assumption that at the micro level, the supply of output would respond to an increase in demand. But the **supply-side** or **monetarist fiscal policy** pursued since 1979 has been completely different. At the macro level, the Conservative Government has subordinated fiscal policy to monetary policy, and has adopted a fiscal policy which the Government believes is consistent with the monetary policy aim of controlling inflation. Meanwhile, at the micro level, fiscal policy has been used, along with other elements of the Conservative Government's economic programme such as privatisation and deregulation, to increase the role of markets and of private sector economic activity and to reduce the economic role of the state. Look at the suggested answer to Question 2 for a more detailed discussion of recent UK fiscal policy.

If you need to revise this subject more thoroughly, see the relevant topics in the *Letts A level Economics Study Guide*.

QUESTIONS

1 (a) Should control of the money supply be an essential part of macroeconomic policy? (60)

(b) Discuss **two** problems that have been encountered in the operation of monetary policy in the UK over the past decade. (40)

ULEAC

2 Distinguish between monetary and fiscal policy. Discuss the role of fiscal policy in the management of the economy by a 'monetarist' government. (25)

AEB

QUESTIONS

3

Nominal interest rate and inflation rate, August 1990 – September 1991

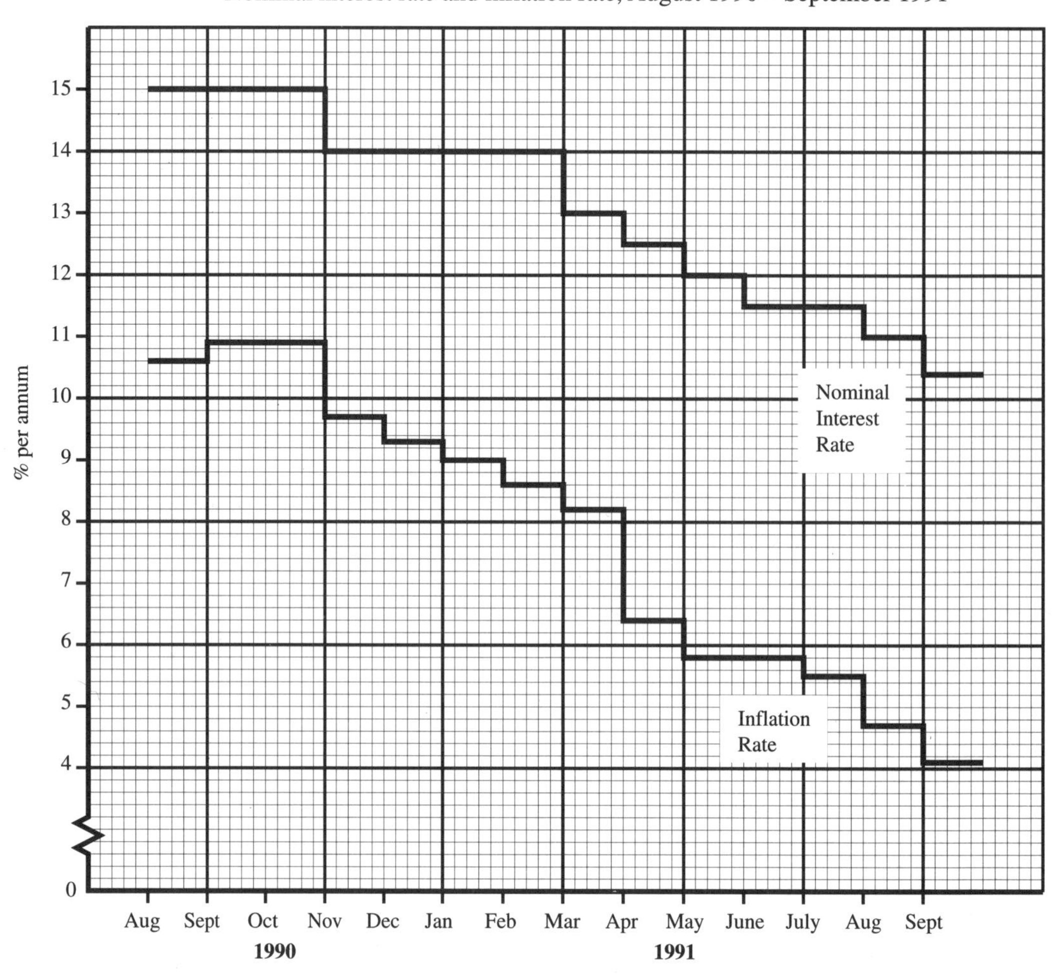

(a) Explain the meaning of the following terms:
 (i) nominal interest rate; (2)
 (ii) inflation rate. (2)

(b) Explain why, in real life, there are several different rates of interest in operation in the UK at any one time. (4)

(c) Explain, fully, how a fall in the nominal interest rate might affect the inflation rate. (4)

(d) (i) Explain briefly **one monetary measure**, other than changes in interest rates, which the UK government could use to attempt to reduce inflation. (2)
 (ii) Explain briefly **two fiscal measures** which the UK government could use to attempt to reduce inflation. (4)

(e) (i) Define the 'real rate of interest' and calculate it for the beginning of April 1991. (2)
 (ii) Why is the real rate of interest of importance to borrowers and savers? (2)

(f) Early in 1992, the UK had higher real rates of interest than its major competitors. What effects would this have on:
 (i) economic growth in the UK; (4)
 (ii) the UK balance of payments? (4)

SEB

The case for free trade

The case for specialisation and trade between countries stems from two important economic principles, the benefits of the division of labour and the principle of comparative advantage. The **benefits of the division of labour** suggest that if each of the world's countries with its own endowment of both natural or 'God-given' resources such as soil, climate and minerals, and 'man-made' resources such as capital, know-how and labour skills, specialises in 'what it does best', total world output or production can be increased compared to a situation without specialisation. By engaging in trade, a country can escape the constraints of limited natural resources and small domestic markets. By importing raw materials, energy, foodstuffs and manufactured consumer goods, the country's industries can produce, and its residents can enjoy, a range of goods and services which its own resource base would not allow. Likewise, access to the wider world market can allow the country's industries to benefit from long production runs and economies of scale in a way that would not be possible if the country relied solely on the domestic market.

A country possesses an **absolute advantage** in an industry if it is technically more efficient at producing a good or service than other countries, i.e. if it produces a greater output from given inputs or resources. Absolute advantage must not be confused with the rather more subtle concept of comparative advantage. **Comparative advantage** is measured in terms of opportunity cost, or what a country gives up when it increases the output of an industry by one unit. The country which gives up the least other goods when increasing output of a commodity by one unit possesses the comparative advantage in that good. Study the numerical example in the answer to Question 1 of this unit to see how specialisation in accordance with the principle of comparative advantage can increase the total output produced by two countries.

Import controls and protectionism

There are four main ways in which a country can control or deter imports, and protect its domestic industries from international competition. These are: (i) **tariffs or import duties** (and **subsidies** for domestically produced goods); (ii) an **undervalued exchange rate**; (iii) **import quotas**; and (iv) artificial barriers such as 'voluntary' export restrictions and **administrative procedures** and **technical standards**. The first two of these protectionist measures raise the relative price of imported goods compared to goods produced within the country. Import quotas impose a maximum limit or ceiling on imports, while the need to meet bureaucratic administrative procedures and technical standards can deter trade by forcing importers to incur extra costs, risk and uncertainty. Refer to the answer to Question 1 for coverage of the economic arguments which might justify import controls.

The terms of trade

The **terms of trade** measure the average price of exports as a ratio of the average price of imports. An increase in the price of exports relative to the price of imports means that one unit of exports can purchase more imports from other countries. This is known as an improvement or favourable movement in the terms of trade. But, by destroying competitiveness, a favourable movement in the terms of trade, caused for example by the country's inflation rate exceeding that of its competitors, may lead to a deterioration in the country's balance of payments. A revaluation or appreciation of the exchange rate also improves the terms of trade, while a devaluation results in a deterioration in the terms of trade.

Free trade areas and customs unions

Free trade areas and customs unions are examples of **trading blocs** and **multilateral trading agreements**. Membership of a **free trade area** requires a country to reduce or eliminate tariffs against other members while being free to choose its own tariffs against non-members. Consequently, a country can belong to two or more free trade areas simultaneously. Similarly, the rules of a **customs union** require the abolition of internal tariffs between members, but unlike a

REVISION SUMMARY

free trade area, all members must adopt a common external tariff aimed against the rest of the world. Membership of a customs union, such as the European Union, is not usually compatible with continued membership of a free trade area.

Exchange rates

An exchange rate is simply the price of a country's currency, measured in terms of another currency, a commodity such as gold, or an artificial unit such as the **European Currency Unit (ECU)**. There are three types of exchange rate system: (i) freely floating; (ii) rigidly fixed; and (iii) managed exchange rate systems. In a **freely floating system**, market forces or supply and demand determine the exchange rate without any government interference. At the other extreme, in a **rigidly fixed system**, the country's central bank buys and sells reserves of gold and other currencies, and also sets interest rates, so as to prevent market forces moving the exchange rate away from the central parity at which it is pegged. There are two **managed systems** between these extremes: (i) an **adjustable peg system**; and (ii) **'managed' floating**. An adjustable peg system resembles a rigidly fixed system, except that a revaluation or devaluation can be used to adjust the peg upwards or downwards if the exchange rate becomes undervalued or overvalued in terms of the country's trading competitiveness. In the 1980s, the **exchange rate mechanism (ERM)** of the **European Monetary System (EMS)** was an adjustable peg system, but by the time the pound joined in 1990, realignments were frowned upon and the ERM had become more like a rigidly fixed system. Since leaving the ERM in 1992, the pound has floated, sometimes freely, but at other times being 'managed'. With managed or 'dirty' floating, the monetary authorities intervene behind the scenes to determine the exchange rate, but without publicly declaring their exchange rate target, or indeed the fact that they are intervening to influence the exchange rate.

Balance of payments problems

The **balance of payments** is the part of a country's National Accounts which measures all the currency flows into and out of the economy within a particular time period, usually a year. The balance of payments on current account measures the flow of expenditure on goods and services, broadly indicating the country's income gained and lost from trade. The **current account**, made up of the **balances of visible and invisible trade**, is usually regarded as the most important part of the balance of payments because it reflects the economy's international competitiveness and the extent to which it is living within its means. Although in an accounting sense the balance of payments must always balance, the country's payments may not be in a state of equilibrium. The balance of payments is in equilibrium when the current account more or less balances over a period of years. **Balance of payments equilibrium** is perfectly compatible with the occurrence of short-term deficits and surpluses. It can also be applied to the current account and the capital account (transactions in assets and liabilities) over a number of years. While a short-run deficit or surplus on current account does not pose a problem, a persistent imbalance indicates a fundamental disequilibrium. However, the nature of any resulting problem depends upon the size and cause of the deficit or surplus, and also upon the type of exchange rate regime. The larger the deficit, the greater the problem is likely to be. The problem is also likely to be serious if the deficit is caused by the uncompetitiveness of the country's industries. In the short run, a deficit allows a country's residents to enjoy living standards which, boosted by imports, are higher than would be possible from the consumption of the country's output alone. In the long run, however, the decline of the country's industries in the face of international competition will lower living standards.

A balance of payments deficit is usually considered more of a problem in a regime of fixed exchange rates than when the exchange rate is freely floating. The immediate cause of a deficit usually lies in the fact that exports are too expensive in overseas markets, while imports are too cheap at home. In theory, a floating exchange rate simply responds to market forces and falls, thereby restoring export competitiveness and curing the balance of payments disequilibrium. By contrast, when the exchange rate is fixed, overvaluation of the exchange rate may occur, which cannot be cured by market forces because in a fixed system, the exchange rate is not allowed to

If you need to revise this subject more thoroughly, see the relevant topics in the ***Letts A level Economics Study Guide.***

REVISION SUMMARY

respond to market forces. In the absence of inward capital flows financing the resulting persistent payments deficit, the country will simply lose official reserves. Official reserves are of course limited, so a country cannot go on financing a deficit for ever. In a fixed exchange rate system, therefore, a country must eventually take action – usually deflation – to try to reduce or eliminate a persistent payments deficit.

QUESTIONS

1 (a) Illustrate how the principle of comparative advantage works to make international trade efficient. (15)

(b) What **economic** reasons exist to restrict world-wide free trade? (10)

Oxford & Cambridge

2 (a) What is 'a deficit on the current account of the balance of payments'? (6)

(b) Does a deficit on current account matter to an economy, particularly during a recession? (14)

Oxford

3

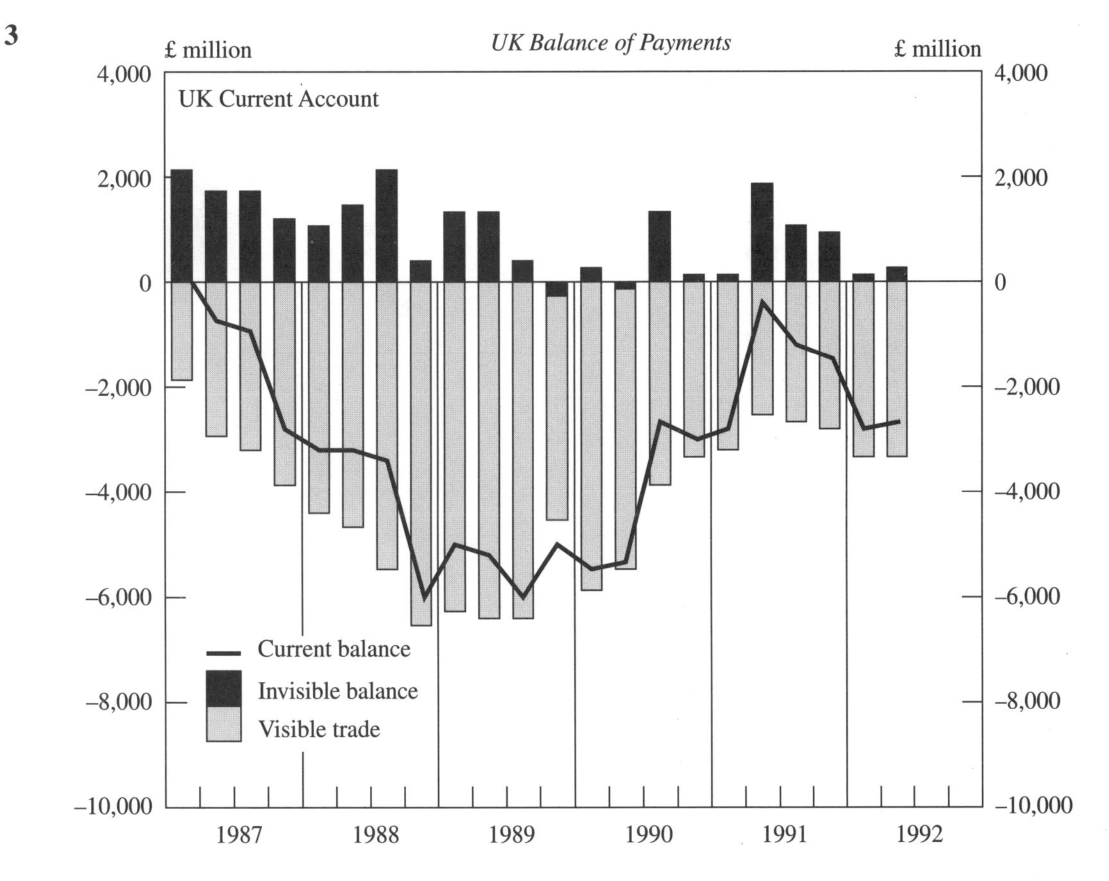

(a) With reference to the diagram:

(i) Distinguish between the 'invisible balance' and 'visible trade'. (3)

(ii) Describe and account for the trend in the UK current balance in the period between 1987 and mid-1992. (5)

QUESTIONS

Table 1

Sterling Exchange Rate Index (1985 = 100) and Selected UK Retail Bank Base Interest Rates, 1987–1991

Year	Sterling Exchange Rate Index (1985 = 100)	Base Rate (%)
1987	90.1	8.50
1988	95.5	13.00
1989	92.6	15.00
1990	91.3	14.00
1991	91.7	10.50

Table 2

Sterling Exchange Rate Index (1985 = 100) and Selected UK Retail Bank Base Interest Rates, Jan–Nov 1992

Month	Sterling Exchange Rate Index (1985 = 100)	Base Rate (%)
Jan	90.8	10.50
Feb	90.8	10.50
Mar	90.1	10.50
Apr	91.3	10.50
May	92.8	10.00
June	92.8	10.00
July	92.5	10.00
Aug	92.0	10.00
Sept	88.2	9.00
Oct	80.8	8.00
Nov	78.3	7.00

Source: *Economic Trends*, December 1992, CSO

(b) (i) Explain possible relationships between the UK current balance, the sterling exchange rate index and bank base interest rates in the period between 1987 and 1991. (6)

(ii) Suggest other factors which may have influenced bank base interest rates during this period. (2)

(c) Give reasons for the fall in both the sterling exchange rate index and bank base interest rates from August to November 1992. (4)

ULEAC

1 ECONOMIC SYSTEMS AND THE MARKET MECHANISM

Answer	Mark

1 (a) A mixed economy can be defined in two ways: in terms of ownership and in terms of the mechanism which allocates scarce resources between competing uses. In terms of ownership of the means of production, a mixed economy can be defined as having a large private sector and a large public sector. The private sector contains private enterprise business organisations, ranging from sole traders and other types of small business to large public companies or PLCs such as British Petroleum, ICI and Marks & Spencer. The public sector represents the state's contribution to economic activity, through its ownership of nationalised industries and through the provision of public services such as education and roads. This brings us to the second characteristic of a mixed economy: the mix between market and non-market economic activity. In the market sector of the economy, the price mechanism allocates scarce resources between competing uses. Private sector businesses (and also nationalised industries) operate largely within the market sector of the economy, selling their output of goods and services commercially for a profit. By contrast, public sector services have traditionally been provided in the non-market sector of the economy, 'free at the point of consumption' to users, and financed collectively out of taxation. **For defining a mixed economy: up to 5 marks**

The extent to which an economy is mixed depends in part upon historical factors and, in a democracy, on what people have voted for at the ballot box. A mixed economy is a pragmatic response to the fact that many, if not most, goods and services can be classified as private goods, which the market is good at providing, but there are a number of market failures. Arguably, the main market failures in a pure market economy include: failure to provide public goods; under-provision of merit goods and positive externalities; over-provision of demerit goods and negative externalities; monopoly and produce sovereignty; 'missing markets'; the tendency for 'short-termism' at the expense of the long-term; inequitable distributions of income and wealth; and unemployment and wasted resources. There is a case for government intervention in the free market system to correct these market failures, while ensuring that the market mechanism is left free to continue to provide private goods in competitive markets.Thus the government provides public goods and merit goods and uses progressive taxation and public spending on welfare benefits to make the distribution of income more fair or equitable.

For explaining resource allocation: up to 10 marks

Examiner's tip

Frequently, candidates define a mixed economy by writing all they know about a market economy, followed by all they know about command economies, and then the statement that 'a mixed economy is defined as being midway between these extremes'. At best such an approach will earn only a low pass mark. It really is important to define a mixed economy in terms of the mix of the sectors that make it up, and if the question requires it, to state the basic reasons for state and non-market provision of goods and services.

(b) For about thirty years after the end of the Second World War, from the 1940s to the 1970s, a large measure of agreement existed in the United Kingdom about the virtues of the mixed economy.

From the 1960s onward, a growing minority of economists and politicians began to blame the mixed economy for Britain's deteriorating economic performance relative to that of its main competitors in Western Europe and Japan.

Free-market economists argue that a mixed economy is less efficient than a pure market economy because of what they see as the burdens imposed upon private enterprise by the activities of the public sector. They believe that the taxation needed to finance public sector non-market provision of goods and services in a market economy creates a burden upon private enterprise firms in the market sector. Some extreme free-market economists have argued that the mixed economy should be broken up completely and replaced by a pure market economy. However, other 'free-marketeers' are less extreme. They accept that the economic roles of the state and the non-market sector are necessary in two areas of economic life: in the production of public goods and merit goods which markets by their nature find difficult to produce or underproduce; and by providing a 'safety net' of welfare benefits for the groups in society such as the old, the handicapped and the long-term unemployed, who otherwise might be the victims of unregulated market forces.

For explaining the alleged need for change: up to 3 marks

The main policies used to change the nature of the mix have been privatisation, marketisation and deregulation. Privatisation has involved the transfer of previously state-owned assets (mostly nationalised industries) to the private sector. In 1979 there were over two dozen nationalised industries; by 1995 most had been sold to private owners and only two or three were left. In contrast to privatisation (which shifts assets from the public sector to the private sector), marketisation (or commercialisation) transfers economic activities from the non-market sector (financed by taxation) to the market sector. Although marketisation has often accompanied privatisation, this has not always been the case. Many services are still provided by the public sector, but a market price is now charged, whereas previously the service was available free or at a purely token charge. Finally, by removing barriers to market entry which had previously protected activities such as municipally run bus services, deregulation has also promoted private enterprise and accelerated the decline of production within the public sector.

For describing how the economy has changed: up to 3 marks

Despite these changes, it is still correct to describe the UK economy as a mixed economy, though the nature of the mix has undoubtedly changed. For example, despite commercialisation and the introduction of an 'internal market' having changed the nature of the National Health Service, the NHS absorbs an increasing share of national resources and the service is still financed predominantly from tax revenue. Likewise, education, the police and defence, and the provision of services such as roads still remain predominantly in the public and non-market sectors, though it is possible that they will be increasingly provided by private enterprise and markets in future years. A pure market economy and a complete shift to private enterprise would require the complete disappearance of public sector and non-market provision, but there appears little chance of this happening.

For concluding whether the UK is still a mixed economy: up to 4 marks

Examiner's tip

You must avoid the temptation simply to describe the present configuration of the UK economy, and you should also indicate how you are interpreting the words 'recent years'. You might consider only the last ten years before the examination: alternatively, it would be reasonable to go back as far as 1979 when Margaret Thatcher's Conservative

administration began the process of changing significantly the structure of the UK economy. The wording of the question clearly indicates that you must show awareness of the changes that have taken place in the UK economy in the recent past. You must explain how government policies, such as privatisation and the introduction of the price mechanism in the provision of many public sector services previously provided free, have wrought significant changes on the UK economy. Make sure to give an opinion as to whether the economy is still a mixed economy. One approach would be to conclude that it is still a mixed economy, but that the nature of the mix has changed.

---

2 (a) Strictly defined, a market economy is an economy in which all economic activity takes place in the system of markets which make up the economy. Usually, however, the term 'market economy' is used in a rather looser way to describe any economy (such as the USA or Switzerland) in which markets are dominant and the role of government in the economy is reduced as much as possible to a minimum. Indeed many 'mixed economies' (such as the UK) at the free-market end of the spectrum between the two extremes of pure command and market economies, are often called market economies. But whichever way a market economy is defined, its key feature is the price mechanism functioning as the main mechanism through which a society's scarce resources are allocated among competing uses.

For defining a market economy: up to 2 marks

In a market economy, prices perform three main functions, known as the signalling, incentive and rationing (or allocative) functions. The signalling function simply means that prices signal what is available, conveying the information which allows all the traders in the market to plan and co-ordinate their economic activities. Markets will function inefficiently, sometimes breaking down completely or leading to 'market failure', if prices signal wrong or misleading information. The information conveyed or signalled by prices then creates incentives for households and firms to behave and make decisions in ways consistent with pursuing and achieving the fulfilment of their private benefit or self-interest. This then leads on to the rationing or allocative function. Working through the incentives created by changing relative prices in different markets, households switch their consumption or demand decisions away from goods which have become relatively more expensive towards relatively cheaper goods. This is called the substitution effect of relative price changes. And if producers or entrepreneurs believe that changing relative prices signal different profit opportunities in different markets, they will switch productive resources from less profitable to more profitable markets. In this way the price mechanism rations or allocates scarce resources between competing uses in a market economy.

For each function listed: 1 mark
For further development: up to 4 marks each

Examiner's tip

The key instruction here is 'explain'. This means that you must develop you answer beyond merely stating the three functions of prices in a market economy. Also make sure you provide a brief explanation of the meaning of a market economy.

(b) Traffic congestion creates a negative externality or external cost, which is an example of a market failure. The market failure arises in large part precisely because, in the past, it has been impossible (or perhaps politically inexpedient) to

use the price mechanism to charge motorists for the traffic congestion they cause and the costs this imposes on other road users. The diagram below shows why congestion caused by motorists is a market failure.

For explaining why congestion is a market failure: up to 5 marks

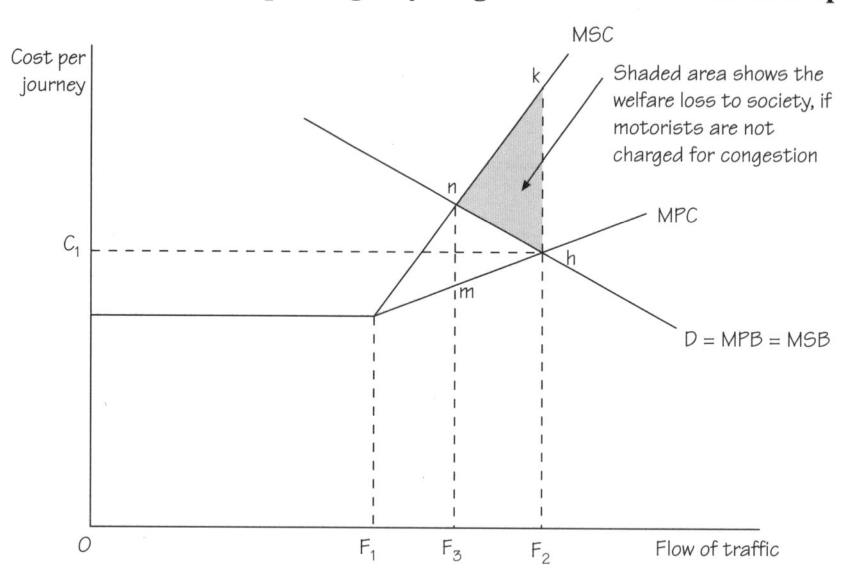

The effect of introducing road pricing

The graph shows the relationship between the cost of travel and the traffic flow along a particular road. We assume that when driving a car, a motorist considers only the marginal private cost (MPC) incurred, which are the costs of time, fuel, and wear and tear resulting from an extra journey. He or she can ignore the costs of congestion imposed on other motorists, which when added to the marginal private cost make up the marginal social cost (MSC) of the journey. Up to a traffic flow of F_1 on the diagram, there is no congestion, and MPC = MSC (assuming no other externalities such as pollution). But as traffic increases above F_1, congestion occurs, creating a divergence between MPC and MSC. Assuming that the demand curve D measures the marginal private benefits (MPB) and the marginal social benefits (MSB) of an extra journey, total traffic flow is determined at F_2, where MPB = MPC. At this point, the private cost to the marginal motorist is C_1, which does not take into account the marginal external cost, represented by the distance hk imposed on other road users. A misallocation of resources is occurring, and motorists are making more journeys than they would if they had to bear the full social cost of any journey they made. The shaded area hkn measures the welfare loss suffered by society at the privately optimal traffic flow F_2.

Hence there is a case for road pricing, such as tolls or electronic pricing. Allocative efficiency can be improved if motorists are made to pay a price equal to the marginal external cost imposed on other road users of each journey. The optimal road price would be equal to mn, which measures the marginal external cost of road use at the socially optimal level of road use, F_3. Some congestion still occurs at F_3, but it is less than at F_2 without road pricing. Marginal journeys, which – in the absence of the road price – would have been undertaken, will no longer be worthwhile. They will not take place at all, or they will be switched to a less congested time of day (assuming that the price charged is based on the degree of congestion), or they might be switched to an alternative route not subject to road pricing.

But road pricing can have disadvantages. The poor might suffer disproportionately. Also, road pricing could simply shift congestion away from previously busy roads to other, previously uncongested and unpriced roads. For example, a pricing system introduced solely on motorways would probably cause traffic to move back onto the ordinary roads the motorways were designed to relieve. To avoid this outcome, road use would have to be priced on all potentially congested roads.The installation of toll gates might be only partially effective in reducing congestion, since queues may build up at the toll gates themselves.

For the case for and against: up to 6 marks

Electronic pricing does not have this disadvantage. Electronic pricing makes it possible to record when and where a car is being driven, and to bill the owner at a later date. It is also easy to charge higher prices on roads at times of maximum congestion. And road pricing has the advantage over the main alternative (regulation or banning motorists from using their cars) because motorists who really want to travel will be prepared to pay the price for using the roads. The price mechanism should encourage motorists whose journeys are less essential to make other arrangements. As noted, they may decide not to travel or they may switch to an alternative method of transport or to a time of day when there is less congestion and hence a lower price charged. **For overall assessment: up to 2 marks**

Examiner's tip

Traffic congestion is an example of a negative externality or external cost, and you must clearly state that this is the case. When, in a market situation, economic agents (such as motorists) produce negative externalities, market failure is likely to occur (see Unit 6 for a more detailed explanation of market failure). Note that using the price mechanism to reduce a market failure might appear to be a contradiction in terms, since resource allocation via the price mechanism has initially led to the market failure occurring! The question asks you to assess the case, so you must conclude with a personal view on whether the advantages of road pricing exceed the disadvantages.

---

3 Examiner's answer plan

(a) (i) Briefly explain the meaning of a free market. **1 mark**

(ii) State that in a free market prices are determined solely by the forces of supply and demand. **1 mark**

(iii) With the aid of a supply and demand diagram for a particular market, explain how the price rises or falls to eliminate any excess demand or supply, thereby attaining an equilibrium. **3 marks**

(iv) Indicate how shifts of supply and demand curves both cause and respond to price changes in different markets. **2 marks**

(b) (i) State that the shape of a demand curve stems ultimately from the assumption of a utility maximising objective on the part of households. **1 mark**

(ii) Explain how a household (or individual consumer) seeks to maximise utility subject to constraints – such as limited income, prices and given tastes and preferences. **1 mark**

(iii) Introduce the law of diminishing marginal utility. **1 mark**

(iv) Consumer equilibrium is achieved when household income is spent so that the condition of equi-marginal utility holds (the ratios of marginal utility to price are equated for all goods). **Up to 2 marks**

(v) If the relative prices of goods change, to maximise utility the household will demand more of the good whose price has fallen and less of goods which have become relatively more expensive. This is the substitution effect of a price change, which is the main factor responsible for demand for a good rising as its price falls. **Up to 3 marks**

(vi) If you have time, note also that for 'normal' goods, the income effect of the price change also contributes to the explanation. **Maximum of 6 marks for part (b)**

(c) (i) State that the factors which affect demand, other than the good's own price, determine the position of the demand curve. **1 mark**

(ii) List and very briefly explain the main factors: disposable income; tastes and preferences; the price of complementary goods and substitutes. **Up to 3 marks**

(iii) Illustrate on a diagram, how a change in one of these 'conditions of demand' shifts the demand curve. **1 mark**

(iv) Argue that, on occasion, some of these non-price factors can cause significant changes in demand. Quote at least two examples: for example, the effect of advertising in boosting the demand for a product such as Coca-Cola, despite its 'premium' price; or an increase in income reducing demand for an 'inferior' good such as public transport. **Up to 4 marks**

(v) Conclude by arguing that nevertheless, a good's price relative to other goods is probably the most important factor influencing demand for most goods most of the time. **Up to 3 marks**

Examiner's tip

For part (a), be sure to explain how the price mechanism relieves excess demand or supply *within* a market and how the price mechanism operates *between* markets as supply and demand curves shift in response to relative price changes.

For part (b), you must introduce a theory of consumer behaviour, for example utility theory. There is a lot which could be written here for only 6 marks, so you must resist the temptation to treat this as a full essay question.

Part (c) requires you to list and briefly explain the 'conditions of demand' which determine the position of a demand curve. But, to earn more than a basic pass mark for this part of the question, you must assess whether these factors may be more important than price, remembering at the same time to base your discussion on at least two examples.

2 ECONOMIC EFFICIENCY AND MARKET STRUCTURE

Answer	Mark

1 (a) The condition set out in the quotation, namely that the price at which a good is sold equals the marginal cost of producing the good ($P = MC$), is the condition which must hold for allocative efficiency to be achieved. The market structure in which this condition always holds is perfect competition.

For identifying the market structure: 1 mark

Perfect competition is a market structure in which each of the very large number of firms in the market can sell whatever quantity of the good it wishes, providing the good is sold at the ruling market price determined in the market as a whole. Each firm is a passive 'price taker' at the ruling market price. If the firm were to raise its selling price above the ruling market price it would lose all its sales, yet it would be irrational to undercut the market price as no extra sales would result, but profits would be reduced. The ruling market price thus represents the firm's average revenue (AR) curve and also its marginal revenue (MR) curve. As in all market structures, the profit-maximising level of output for each firm occurs at the level of output at which MR = MC. It follows that since, in perfect competition, P = MR, P must also equal MC when the firm is producing the profit-maximising level of output.

For explaining why P = MC: up to 6 marks

The obvious starting point for explaining why perfect competition, as a market structure, is advantageous for consumers, is the concept of allocative efficiency itself. The price of a good, P, is a measure of the value in consumption placed by buyers on the last unit consumed, indicating the utility or welfare obtained at the margin in consumption. If P > MC, households pay a price for the last unit consumed which is greater than the cost of producing the last unit. The high price discourages consumption, so we conclude that at this price the good is under-produced and under-consumed. Conversely, when P < MC, the value (P) placed on the last unit consumed by households is less than the MC of the resources used to produce the last unit. The price is too low, encouraging too much consumption of the good. Thus at this price the good is over-produced and over-consumed. A reallocation of resources between markets from the second group of markets where P < MC to the former group in which P > MC, enables total consumer welfare or utility to increase. As the reallocation proceeds, prices will fall in those markets into which resources are being shifted and rise in the markets from which resources are being moved. Eventually P will equal MC in all markets. Beyond the point at which P = MC in all markets, no further reallocation of resources between markets can improve consumer welfare, *ceteris paribus*. If all the markets in the economy were perfectly competitive, the 'hidden hand' of the market would achieve an efficient allocation of the economy's resources between markets, providing we assume an absence of externalities and economies of scale.

For explaining why consumers benefit: up to 7 marks

Examiner's tip

The question requires you to identify a particular market structure *before* explaining how the market structure benefits consumers. It is not necessary to explain in detail the conditions of perfect competition, or to derive from first principles the shapes of a perfectly competitive firm's cost and revenue curves. But do make sure to draw on the quotation at the beginning of the question. It should signal to you that you must show how consumers benefit from the concept of economic efficiency.

(b) One market structure in which the condition that P = MC does not apply is monopoly. In monopoly equilibrium, and producing at the level of output at which MR = MC, the price charged is greater than marginal cost (P > MC). This means that the price is too high, discouraging consumption, and the market structure is allocatively inefficient. In the absence of economies of scale, monopoly equilibrium is also productively inefficient because the level of output at which MR = MC is very unlikely to be the one at which average costs are minimised. The monopolist produces a level of output which is not at the lowest point on the AC curve. It is

also quite likely that a monopolist will be X-inefficient, incurring unnecessary costs of production and failing to maximise profits. X-inefficiency can occur if the monopolist is content with satisfactory profits rather than the highest possible profits, i.e. if the monopolist is a profit *satisficer* rather than a profit *maximiser*. Barriers to entry and a lack of competitive pressure may also promote X-inefficiency in a monopoly market structure. **For identifying the market structure: 1 mark**

For explaining why P > MC: up to 4 marks

For explaining resulting inefficiencies: up to 6 marks

The fact that the price charged by a monopolist is greater than the marginal cost of production may also be judged inequitable or unjust. This is because the monopolist's customers gain less consumer surplus (which is a measure of economic welfare) than would be the case if the price were lower. Most of the consumer surplus which is removed from consumers boosts monopoly profits. But a net welfare loss also results, because part of the consumer surplus removed from consumers simply disappears in the sense that nobody now benefits from it.

For explaining how equity is impaired: up to 5 marks

Examiner's tip

You would be correct to choose any market structure *other* than perfect competition, for example monopolistic competition, oligopoly or duopoly. However, it is probably best to choose monopoly, because this is the least difficult to analyse in terms of efficiency. Note that the question also asks you to discuss equity. You must do this, however briefly, in order to have a chance of earning full marks.

---

2 Examiner's answer plan

(a) (i) Define absolute monopoly as one firm only in a market. **1 mark**

(ii) Draw, and explain briefly, a diagram to show a profit-maximising monopoly, making sure you clearly show that profits are maximised at the level of output where MR = MC. **Up to 5 marks**

(iii) Explain that for the monopolist, MR < AR, and that barriers to market entry protect the supernormal profits made by the monopoly. **Up to 2 marks**

(b) (i) Make the general point that control of monopoly is desirable if the costs of monopoly (for the whole community) exceed the benefits. **Up to 2 marks**

(ii) Explain the various costs of monopoly: raising the price and restricting output; restriction of choice; producer sovereignty at the expense of consumer sovereignty; productive, allocative and X-inefficiencies. **Up to 4 marks**

(iii) Explain the possible benefits of monopoly: productive efficiency gains through economies of scale; dynamic efficiency gains. **Up to 4 marks**

(iv) Conclude by explaining that any appropriate form of control, such as regulation, should attempt to promote the benefits of monopoly while minimising the costs. **Up to 2 marks**

Examiner's tip

For part (a), you should define monopoly and draw a diagram to show a profit-maximising monopolist. Once again, don't bother to explain all the cost and revenue curves in detail, but do explain that the (downward-sloping) market demand curve is the monopolist's average revenue curve, and that the marginal revenue curve lies below the AR curve. For

part (b), you must explain how, compared to perfect competition, a monopolist is inefficient, restricting output and raising price, though monopolies can benefit from economies of scale and dynamic efficiency. Make sure you apply specific efficiency concepts such as productive, allocative and dynamic efficiency. Take note of the mark allocation. Your answer to part (b) should be developed more than that for part (a).

---

3 (a) (i) Dynamic efficiency means gains in efficiency that occur through time, as new and better methods are developed for producing existing products, and completely new products are devised. **2 marks**

(ii) Static efficiency refers to improvements in resource allocation (allocative efficiency gains) and economies in resource utilisation (technical and productive efficiency gains) that can be made, given the state of technical knowledge, i.e. assuming no technical progress. **2 marks**

(iii) Monopoly power refers to the ability of established firms in a market to restrict output and choice and market entry, and to raise prices. **2 marks**

Examiner's tip

The important point with this question is to make sure you obey the instruction to 'explain in your own words'. Simply copying out the data will not earn any marks.

(b) (i) Whereas 'invention' refers to advances in pure science, 'innovation' is the application of invention or scientific developments to production. Increases in market size might increase innovation in at least three ways. Firstly, many innovations require the long production runs which large market size permits. Secondly, large market size holds out the promise of larger future profits, which may provide the incentive for firms to undertake more product development. Thirdly, large European-wide markets may be more competitive than smaller, strictly national markets; firms may need to innovate in order to survive.

Defining innovation: 1 mark

Explaining why large market may promote innovation: up to 4 marks

(ii) Patent legislation provides support for the proposition that 'large firms with at least some degree of monopoly power are likely to be the most innovative'. Patent law gives a firm the legal monopoly to enjoy the fruits of its innovation for a number of years, thereby creating the incentive to innovate. Arguably, if there were no patent law, the incentive to innovate would disappear, because firms would fear that their competitors would 'free-ride', i.e. wait for a pioneering firm to innovate, then steal the knowledge without incurring the research and development costs. **Up to 5 marks**

Examiner's tip

Make sure you explain what is meant by 'innovation'.

(c) The European Community (or European Union as it is now called) is an example of a customs union. This means that, with one or two exceptions (for example, the protection of newly established industries in the poorer EU countries), all member countries have abolished trade barriers within the union, while accepting a common

external tariff imposed on imports from non-members. As the passage indicates, member countries may expect to benefit in a number of ways. The main points made in the passage are: (i) firms in member countries should benefit from static efficiency gains in the form of lower costs brought about by attaining economies of scale, which in turn are possible because of access to a larger market; and (ii) consumers may eventually benefit from increased innovation brought about by increased competition in the larger market. However in the author's view, monopoly rather than competition is more likely to produce such a gain in dynamic efficiency. The author believes that membership of the European Community can result in a net increase in efficiency for member countries, but this outcome may depend on whether the gains in static efficiency exceed a possible loss in dynamic efficiency.

For outlining how the EU has removed trade barriers: up to 2 marks
For explaining the gains: up to 5 marks

The author of the passage does not discuss whether, if gains occur, they will be shared by *all* member states. Free trade may result in economic decline in European regions (and possibly whole countries) which are unable to compete in an enlarged market. The experience of some of the poorer states in the USA lends some support to this argument. With this in mind, it is useful to remember that the European Union is not just a customs union; many common economic policies are involved, and the Union's supporters intend that the community develops into a full economic union with a single currency. The latter might exacerbate regional divergence within the Union, because weaker countries would not be able to devalue their exchange rates to increase their trading competitiveness. Complete freedom of movement of capital and labour may also lead to regional decline, as capital and labour could migrate to the more prosperous parts of the Union. But other common policies might have the opposite effect, for example EU financial assistance to the poorer regions could redistribute the gains achieved from the common market. Finally, it is worth noting that some pro-market supporters of free trade argue that common policies, such as proposed minimum legal wages within the Union, may make Europe uncompetitive in the wider world market. They might argue that the gains from tariff-free trade set out in the article may disappear in future years as the EU suffers from high production costs and an overprotected labour force.

For discussing counter-arguments: up to 2 marks

Examiner's tip

Part (c) is typical of the final part of many data questions in that, unlike the earlier parts of the question, this part allows you to veer away from the actual content of the passage. Although the content of the passage should help you to write a better answer, you are not required to respond solely to the information in the passage. Do, however, make it clear when and if you use an argument which is made by the author of the passage.

3 COMPETITIVE STRATEGIES IN OLIGOPOLISTIC MARKETS

Answer	Mark

1 **(a)** Competitive oligopoly exists when the rival firms are interdependent in the sense that they must take account of the reactions of one another when forming a market strategy, but independent in the sense that they decide the market strategy without co-operation or collusion. The existence of uncertainty is a characteristic of competitive oligopoly; a firm can never be completely certain of how rivals will react to its marketing strategy. Uncertainty can be reduced and perhaps eliminated by the rivals co-operating or colluding together to fix prices, or output, or even by allocating customers to particular members of the oligopoly. If the oligopolists collude to fix price and output in a cartel agreement or price ring, they behave effectively as a single monopolist. Oligopolists have an incentive to behave in this way because, in terms of joint-profit maximisation and an easier life, the firms can achieve a better outcome for all of them by acting collectively rather than by remaining a competitive oligopoly. On a world-wide scale, cartel agreements are also common amongst governments or producers' associations in primary-producing countries, covering commodities such as oil, tin and coffee.

For explaining the meaning of collusion: up to 2 marks
Examples: up to 2 marks
For explaining reasons for collusion: up to 6 marks

Examiner's tip

Make sure to relate your answers to the firm's business objectives. Emphasise the point that firms may wish to collude because it is in their self-interest, defined in terms of such objectives as profit maximisation, or the enjoyment of an easy life.

(b) If the aim is to increase profits by exploiting consumers, collusion will be against the public interest. When oligopolists collude together to rig the market, they seldom integrate their productive plant at a technical level or engage in joint ventures in research and development. As a result, technical economies of scale and cost-cutting are not achieved. Collusive oligopoly thus tends to produce the familiar disadvantages of monopoly, such as restricted output, increased price, productive and allocative inefficiency, producer sovereignty and loss of consumer choice, without achieving the main benefit and ultimate justification of monopoly, i.e. economies of scale. Indeed, cartel agreements are often designed to keep the least efficient firms in business, thereby reducing the ability of the economy to adapt or rationalise its productive structure to meet changed demand or cost conditions.

For these reasons, collusive oligopolistic arrangements such as cartel agreements are normally illegal, being regarded by governments as against the public interest. However, covert or illicit collusion amongst oligopolists undoubtedly often occurs because, for the reasons already noted, such co-operative behaviour is very much in the interest of individual firms. On occasion, governments actively promote cartel arrangements to protect employment or to try to ensure an 'orderly decline' or rationalisation of an industry such as steel, which may be suffering from over-capacity in the face of international competition. Collusion can be in the public interest if it takes the form of co-operation to improve quality or safety standards.

For interpreting the public interest: up to 3 marks
For explaining why collusion is against the public interest: up to 7 marks

Examiner's tip

You could start off by explaining what you understand by the 'public interest', but devote most of your answer to explaining why collective agreements by firms may not be in the public interest, even though collusion can be in the self-interest of the firms.

(c) Collusive agreements tend to break down for three main reasons. Firstly, as mentioned in the answer to the previous part of the question, governments normally pass laws which make collusive agreements illegal. Government agencies such as the Office of Fair Trading and the Restrictive Practices Court break up any covert or undercover agreements which they discover. Secondly, firms which are not members of the cartel may undercut the cartel's price, causing it to disintegrate. Thirdly, the cartel's price may be undercut if a cartel member cheats on the agreement. This is especially likely when a cartel artificially restricts output in order to force up the price charged. Because of their international nature, attempts to fix the price of primary products by member countries accepting a quota and agreeing not to sell below the cartel price, are especially difficult to sustain. A cartel member faces a temptation to renege on the agreement, or to cheat on the other members, by secretly reducing his price and 'unofficially' selling an output greater than the quota agreed by the cartel. **Up to 3 marks per reason, maximum of 5 marks**

Examiner's tip

Notice that the question is worded in the plural, so you must introduce more than one reason why collusive agreements tend to break down. Quote real world examples if you can.

---

2 (a) A firm may charge different prices for the same product because it is implementing a policy of price discrimination in order to maximise profits. Strictly, a firm engages in price discrimination only when different prices are charged to different customers for the same good or service, for reasons not based on differences in supply costs. Price discrimination normally occurs when a firm possessing a degree of monopoly power divides the market into two or more groups of customers with different elasticities of demand. In order for the firm to undertake price discrimination successfully, it must be possible to identify different groups of customers or markets for the product. This is possible when customers differ in their knowledge of the market or in their ability to 'shop around'. Also, the different groups of customers must have different elasticities of demand. Total profits will be maximised by charging a higher price in a market in which demand is less elastic at any particular price. Finally, the markets must be separated to prevent seepage. Seepage takes place when customers who buy at the lower price in one market resell in the other market at a price which undercuts the oligopolist's price.

Implicit in the above analysis is the assumption that the firm has a profit-maximising objective. Given this assumption, price discrimination is in a firm's interest as it increases profits by transferring consumer surplus away from the firm's customers. **For relating pricing to the firm's objectives: 2 marks**

For explaining the theory of price discrimination: up to 7 marks

For other factors that contribute to different prices: up to 6 marks

Examiner's tip

The question does not refer explicitly to price discrimination, but the theory of price discrimination should provide the main part of the answer. However, you might also mention that firms sometimes incur different costs for supplying an otherwise uniform product to different customers, for example at different times of day or season, or because the customers purchase different quantities or live in different geographical locations. In this situation, the different prices charged may reflect different costs of supply.

(b) Price discrimination is a form of monopoly or oligopoly abuse, exploiting the consumer by reducing or eliminating consumer surplus, which is transferred to the firm charging the discriminatory prices, boosting the firm's supernormal or monopoly profit. Nevertheless, there may be circumstances in which consumers benefit from price discrimination. In the limiting case of price discrimination, the firm charges each customer the maximum price the particular consumer is prepared to pay. Each customer may end up paying a different price. In this situation, the firm's demand curve is its marginal revenue (MR) curve as well as its average revenue (AR) curve. In the absence of price discrimination all customers would pay the price P_1 in the following diagram, and the firm would sell an output of Q_1.

For relating the consumers' interest to consumer surplus: 2 marks
For explaining that the pricing policy is usually against the consumers' interest: up to 3 marks

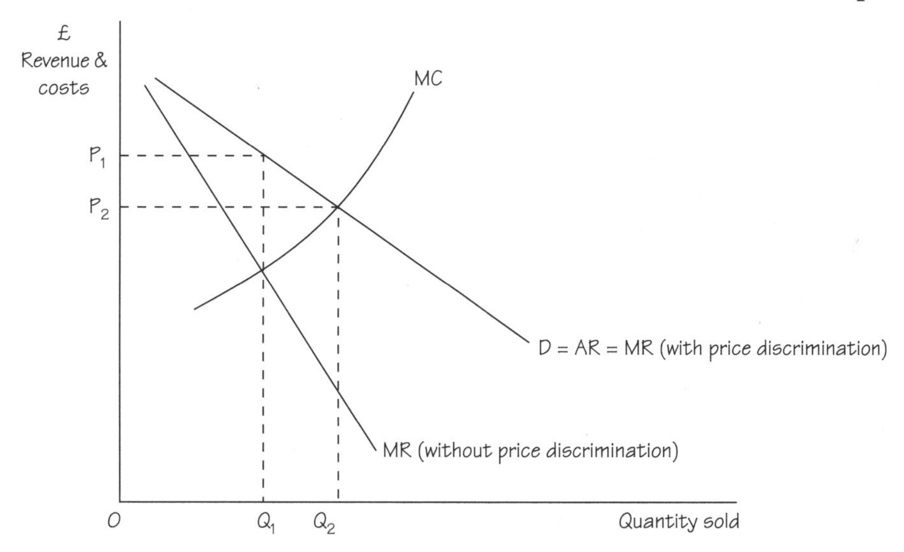

However, with price discrimination (and with the MR curve now being the same as the AR curve), the profit maximising level of output (where MR = MC) increases to Q_2. Also, some (but not all) customers benefit from prices which are lower than P_1; indeed at least one customer (the marginal customer) buys the good at P_2 which is considerably lower than P_1.

Customers might also benefit in circumstances in which firms are unable to make sufficient profit to stay in business without some transfer of consumer surplus from customers to producers. A commonly quoted example concerns the demand for a doctor's services in an isolated small community. When charging the same price to all his patients, the doctor cannot make a large enough income to cover his opportunity cost. He is thus tempted to move to a larger city, thereby leaving the community without medical care. But if he charges each patient a price based on the individual's ability and willingness to pay, he can make sufficient income from

treating the well-off to make it worthwhile to treat the poor at a lower price than the 'market price' that would have been charged in the absence of price discrimination. In this way, everybody gets some benefit and a needed service is provided.

Because price discrimination involves a net loss of consumer surplus and an increase in producer's profit, it is not usually in the interest of the firm's customers taken as a whole. Individual customers, however, may benefit and, as the above example shows, there may be circumstances in which a useful service would not be provided at all unless the supplier can charge discriminatory prices.

For explaining how it may be in the consumers' interest: up to 5 marks

Examiner's tip

You must indicate at least one reason why price discrimination may be against the customers' interest, and one way in which customers may sometimes benefit. Conclude with an overall assessment as to whether there is a net gain or loss for consumers.

---

3 (a) Since only four cross-Channel travel operators are shown in the table, it can be concluded that the market is an oligopoly. An oligopoly is defined as a market in which there are only a few firms. Oligopolists are also interdependent in the sense that they react to each other's pricing and output decisions. It can be inferred from the statement by the Eurotunnel spokesman quoted in Extract A that Eurotunnel is taking account of the prices announced by the ferry companies when setting its own prices. This further supports the view that the market is oligopolistic. There are, however, other cross-Channel operators such as Seacat and the Sally Line not shown in the table, together of course with the airlines. Nevertheless, even if these are taken into account, the market is still a competitive oligopoly.

For stating the market structure: 1 mark
For explanation: up to 2 marks

Examiner's tip

It is insufficient simply to state that the market is oligopolistic; such a basic answer will earn only 1 of the 3 available marks. To earn more than 1 mark, you must explain your reasons.

This is an example of a type of data question which all the examination boards set, based on extracts from topical articles in newspapers about a 'real world' competitive situation. Part (b) of the question is testing your knowledge of price discrimination, and you might also be able to introduce some relevant discussion of marginal cost pricing into this part of your answer. As well as figuring in data questions such as this one, the topic of price discrimination crops up frequently in essay questions.

(b) The table shows that prices are significantly cheaper in off-peak travel times. For example the price of £338 charged by Hoverspeed for a summer peak weekend crossing is more than double the £142 charged during the winter off-peak. The differences between Eurotunnel's peak and off-peak prices are not as great as those for the ferry companies. The reason for this might be that the ferry companies are badly affected by adverse winter weather conditions. Eurotunnel expects to gain more passengers in winter despite higher fares than the ferry companies, because people do not want to travel by sea during winter.

Overall, the differences between peak and off-peak prices can be explained, at least in part, by marginal cost pricing. At peak times, capacity is fully used. The marginal cost of investing in extra capacity to meet any further increase in demand is therefore high. Conversely, in the off-peak, the marginal cost of meeting any extra demand is low because there is plenty of underutilised capacity. There is a case for setting prices based on these differences in marginal costs of supply to promote more efficient use of productive capacity by ironing out differences in demand between the peak and the off-peak. **For marginal cost pricing: up to 3 marks**

There might also be an element of price discrimination in the prices charged. In any market, firms will charge different prices to different customers if, by so doing, they can increase profits. The cross-Channel operators may be acting as price-discriminating oligopolists, charging different prices to different customers on the basis of differences in demand between summer and winter. Passengers travelling in the summer months may be prepared to pay higher prices than those travelling during winter. Having arranged a motoring holiday in Europe, summer passengers may be 'captive' compared to winter passengers. Demand in the summer months may be relatively price-inelastic compared to demand in winter, allowing higher prices to be charged. **For price discrimination: up to 3 marks**

Examiner's tip

First, briefly describe the main features of the pricing differences, before going on to apply economic theory (the theory of price discrimination, possibly supplemented by the theory of marginal cost pricing) to explain these differences. But note that this part of the question carries only 6 marks, whereas parts (c) and (d) have a combined total of 26 marks. There is a danger of 'overwriting' your answer to part (b) and writing too little on parts (c) and (d). Also, avoid mentioning the accurate but irrelevant 'fact' that the delay in opening the Channel Tunnel in 1994 meant that the prices announced by Eurotunnel in January 1994 were never actually charged!

(c) The information in Extract A indicates that at the time of its proposed opening, Eurotunnel was aiming for a market share of 40% of a total market which was then 20 million passengers a year. And if its official announcement that 'there would be no price war' is to be believed, Eurotunnel was aiming to increase its share of the market from 0% to 40%, while, for the most part, charging higher prices than those of its competitors, the ferry companies. The company was not intending to use price competition as the basis of its strategy for winning market share. In the absence of a price war, Eurotunnel might realistically hope to gain 8 million passengers under two sets of circumstances.

In the first place, Eurotunnel is offering a product that is qualitatively different from that of the ferry companies. The differences are speed, possible greater safety and the 'novelty' factor. The fact that Le Shuttle crosses the Channel in a significantly shorter time than the ferries is likely to attract some passengers from the ferries despite the generally higher prices. It has also been argued (though this a matter of hot contention) that the Channel tunnel is safer than a ferry crossing. If passengers believe that Le Shuttle is safer and more comfortable than the ferries, another fraction will switch away from the sea crossing. The safety factor may also increase the competitiveness of Eurotunnel in a different way in future years. If, in response to a number of recent ferry disasters involving loss of life, the ferry companies have to undertake expensive investment to make their ships safer, they may be forced to raise prices. This could eventually give Eurotunnel a price

advantage. Finally, there will undoubtedly be a 'novelty' factor which attracts customers in the first months and years of the tunnel's operation, though Eurotunnel will need to ensure that the service it offers is so good that passengers will be prepared to use Le Shuttle again.

For discussing winning market share: up to 5 marks

Secondly, Eurotunnel may hope to carry 8 million passengers, not only by gaining market share at the expense of the ferry companies, but also because the overall cross-Channel market grows at a very fast rate. The writer of Extract A states rather pessimistically that 'there is little reason to think that there will be any large increase in the volume of traffic carried'. However, this assertion is not backed up by any argument. Indeed, the assertion might be countered with the argument that cross-Channel travel in general – and the Eurotunnel service in particular – is a luxury good, for which demand rises with real income, but at a faster rate. Thus if the economies of the UK and continental countries continue to grow at about 3% to 4% a year, overall demand for cross-Channel travel may grow by say 6% a year. This growth could be further fuelled by cuts in the real cost of cross-Channel travel, which as Extract A says, 'has been falling by 3 to 4 per cent annually for years', even before the possibility of a price war triggered by the entry of Eurotunnel into the market. **For discussing total market growth: up to 5 marks**

On these assumptions, and ignoring the likelihood of a price war, Eurotunnel might hope realistically to gain 8 million passengers, though not necessarily 40% of an expanding market. And a price war would lead to growth in passenger traffic additional to the 3 or 4 per cent a year mentioned in the passage, though not to growth of profits. Other factors which could contribute to Eurotunnel's passenger growth are the continuing economic integration of EU countries, and the growth in popularity of short-stay shopping trips across the Channel, for example the so-called 'booze runs' which take advantage of the lower prices of alcoholic drink in France. But if the economies of Europe enter recession, if Eurotunnel falls victim to disasters, or if the ferry companies find they can cut their prices more aggressively than Eurotunnel, it may prove impossible for Eurotunnel to gain as many as 8 million passengers a year. **For overall assessment: up to 3 marks**

Examiner's tip

You could organise your answer on two assumptions: firstly, that the prices charged by the cross-Channel operators remain as shown in the table, and secondly, that Eurotunnel reduced its prices significantly in order to gain sales. Make sure you reach a conclusion, albeit qualified with 'ifs' and 'buts', on whether you consider it realistic for Eurotunnel to gain 8 million car passengers.

(d) It would be in the interests of all of the cross-Channel travel operators to engage in a price war if the outcome helped to promote their business objectives. Conversely, if the outcome were inconsistent with their business objectives, a price war would not be advantageous. In economic theory, it is usually assumed that all businesses have profit maximisation as their sole objective, though maximising market share is another possible objective. It is conceivable that the price war might increase the sales revenue of all the operators more than their costs, and hence increase their profits – but this is unlikely. The price war might lead to a reduction in sales revenue, which, as costs would undoubtedly increase due to the greater number of passengers to be accommodated, would cut profits and possibly result in losses being made. **For relating price war to business objectives: up to 3 marks**

A business may also start a price war because it believes it will end up a 'winner', gaining both profits and market share at the expense of the 'losers' in the long run. In the short run, and while the price war is taking place, a firm may deliberately forego profit maximisation, perhaps undertaking predatory pricing by deliberately setting price below cost and making a loss, so as to drive competitors out of business. The company hopes that once the price war has been won, its enhanced monopoly position in the market will enable prices to be raised so as to recoup the profits sacrificed during the period of conflict. A price war may be consistent with long-term profit maximisation but not short-term profit maximisation, but only for the victors. **For distinction between short-run and long-run: up to 4 marks**

Thus, while it may not be in the collective interest of the cross-Channel travel operators to undertake a price war, this is not necessarily true for individual operators. As Extract A indicates, even before Eurotunnel began operations the ferry operators suffered from overcapacity. Allowing for market growth, this overcapacity will be made worse by the entry of Eurotunnel into the market. A price war would be likely to force at least one of the 'losing' ferry companies out of the cross-Channel market, perhaps via a merger with the victor. A price war could also force Eurotunnel out of business, but it would be unlikely to close the Channel tunnel. The construction of the Channel tunnel was financed partly through borrowed funds. In order to stay in business, Eurotunnel must earn sufficient sales revenue to enable interest to be paid on these borrowed funds. A price war could lead to a situation in which Eurotunnel would be unable to service its debt and the company might then be forced into liquidation. In these circumstances, Eurotunnel's main asset – the Channel tunnel – might be bought at a 'knockdown price' by another company. The new owner of the tunnel would then be at a competitive advantage *vis-à-vis* the ferry companies because it would not need to service the burden of debt accumulated by Eurotunnel. Under this scenario, the new tunnel operator would be able to cut prices significantly below those charged by the ferry companies so as to gain market share at their expense. In the short term, the ferry companies (considered collectively) might gain from a price war undertaken against Eurotunnel, only to lose in the longer term if the price war led to a change of ownership for the Channel tunnel.

For relevant discussion of winners and losers: up to 6 marks

Examiner's tip

The key instruction here is to 'evaluate'. This means that you must set out the disadvantages of a price war, and then discuss whether these disadvantages are greater than any possible gain to the eventual victor(s) of the price war. Make sure you consider both the short run and the long run, and also avoid drifting into a discussion of advantages and disadvantages for passengers which, though interesting, is irrelevant.

4 ECONOMIES OF SCALE AND INDUSTRIAL CHANGE

Answer **Mark**

1 Economies of scale can be defined as falling long-run average costs of production resulting from the increased size of a plant or firm. In industries such as automobile manufacturing, where there are substantial technical economies of scale associated with the use of expensive capital equipment in assembly line production and long production runs, large firms benefit from significant cost advantages over small firms. Usually, therefore, such industries are dominated by large firms.

Even in such industries, however, there may be a number of specialised market 'niches' (for example in the sports car market), where small firms can survive profitably while incurring higher unit costs because, for example, their customers are prepared to pay a price premium for a customised product. Another factor that has led to the survival of small firms in industries where there are economies of scale, has been the trend to 'contracting out' or 'outsourcing' the supply of services such as security and cleaning, instead of performing them 'in-house'. In other industries, such as the supply of personal services (hairdressing, for instance), there may be economies of small-scale production, rather than economies of scale, which of course encourages the growth of small rather than large business organisations. Also, in recent years the growth of the small firm sector in the UK has been encouraged by the Conservative Government. The Government has created various financial incentives to assist the growth of small firms. An example of a financial measure which promotes the growth of small firms is the Enterprise Allowance Scheme. This created an incentive for the unemployed to seek self-employment without suffering a financial penalty which the loss of unemployment benefit would otherwise have entailed. Financial incentives for small firms and other policy measures to promote 'start-up' businesses reflect the Government's belief in the virtues of 'popular capitalism' and the spread of entrepreneurship in an 'enterprise economy'. At times, these incentives for small firms have also been a response to a general disenchantment with the performance of large firms, particularly in the manufacturing sector. The Conservative Government believes that small firms are more effective than large firms in job creation, since they tend to be more labour intensive. It has also argued that small firms are a major source of technical innovation, and they are more cost-effective than large firms in their research and development. Many new technologies appear to suit small-scale enterprise, since they are less dependent than older technologies upon economies of large-scale production and long production runs.

For explaining economies of scale: up to 6 marks
For arguing that economies of scale may not be significant: up to 6 marks

Indeed, some new technologies in the field of information technology have been developed initially, not by established giants such as IBM, but by completely new 'start-up' businesses founded by university research workers or by employees of the established large companies who decide to leave and set up on their own. In the United States, the Hewlett-Packard electronic instruments company is the classic example of a 'start-up' firm that has grown into a large business with world-wide operations. The company remains a leading firm in the industry that it virtually founded.

The establishment of worker co-operatives and the spread of franchising and management buy-outs have also contributed to the growth of the small firm in the UK. The Co-operative Development Agency and more than 70 local co-operative development agencies assist workers in setting up and running co-operatives. The rapid growth of small worker co-operatives in the 1980s was in large part a response to the depressed

state (at the time) of the economy and growing unemployment. Newly laid-off workers in industries such as engineering decided to form their own co-operatives so that they could continue to work in activities in which they were skilled. At the same time, many newly-unemployed workers entered self-employment as sole traders in activities such as window-cleaning and painting and decorating, as an alternative to the dole. For similar reasons, the rapid growth of unemployment in the recession at the beginning of the 1990s contributed to the growth of small firms. In an economic boom many small 'start-up' businesses grow into medium-sized or even large enterprises, but recession often kills off a fraction of the small businesses founded a few years earlier. It also accelerates the decline and 'death' of previously large businesses which, through a process of structural decline, also qualify as small businesses (albeit of the 'sunset' rather than the 'sunrise' variety), having shrunk to a rump of their former size.

Franchising has become common in the fields of retailing and catering where an individual operates his or her own business, but trades under the franchiser's name and sells the franchiser's products or services. The Kentucky Fried Chicken, or KFC, chain is an example. The individual proprietor holding a franchise typically requires about £25,000 to £30,000 to start up business. He or she must pay the franchiser an annual royalty payment in return for trading under the franchiser's brand name and for receiving the benefits of national advertising and a back-up service. By enabling the franchisee to share in the benefits of economies of scale of the much larger franchising company, franchising encourages the proliferation of small businesses.

Reasons for small firms: up to 4 marks each (maximum of 13 marks)

Examiner's tip

The question starts with an assertion that economies of scale are significant, but you don't have to take this as a proven fact. Possibly the best way to answer the question is to explain briefly what economies of scale are, then to argue that economies of scale are significant in some industries but not in others, before covering in some detail the various explanations for the growth and survival of small firms. However, make sure you don't rewrite the question as 'write all you know about economies of scale and small businesses'.

---

2 (a) The relative decline of manufacturing industry in the UK has been occurring for a period that extends back much further than 1979. Thus the share of national output and employment accounted for by manufacturing fell from 36 and 39 per cent respectively in 1960, to 22 and 23 per cent in 1990. In the pre-1979 period, manufacturing output (and employment) were both growing, but relative decline nevertheless occurred for the simple reason that output and employment in service industries (the tertiary sector) were growing faster. The critical difference for the years after 1979 has been that for two significant periods, the severe recessions of the early 1980s and the early 1990s, absolute as well as relative decline of manufacturing occurred. (*Absolute* decline means that the total output of manufacturing industry falls, whereas *relative* decline means only that the importance of manufacturing compared to other sectors is diminishing. Matters are further complicated by the fact that technical progress tends to favour capital-intensive methods of producing output. Thus, as manufacturing industries such as publishing switch to automated ways of producing books and newspapers, employment falls while output increases in absolute terms.)

For distinguishing between relative and absolute change: up to 10 marks

A number of factors may have contributed to the relative decline of manufacturing. Firstly, the UK has not been alone in suffering a relative (and sometimes absolute) decline of manufacturing. All the older mature industrialised countries of the First World in North America and Western Europe have experienced such a decline. As already noted, the relative decline is in part simply a reflection of the growth of the service sector – if one sector of the economy grows in proportionate importance, then at least one other sector must have fallen proportionately.

However, the fall in the importance of manufacturing in all these older industrialised countries also reflects a shift of manufacturing industry to the newly industrialising countries of the Third World. International trade theory may help to explain this. Comparative advantage in manufacturing, which previously favoured the already-industrialised countries, may now lie with countries such as South Korea, Taiwan and Malaysia. At the same time, as part of the phenomenon known as 'globalisation', manufacturing industry has become 'footloose' on a world scale. Multinational manufacturing companies have closed down their factories in countries such as the UK and switched production to the NICs, sometimes to wholly-owned subsidiaries located in the Third World, but also by 'contacting out' production to indigenous local manufacturing firms.

For each reason: up to 15 marks (maximum of 45 marks)

In the case of Britain, other factors may have contributed to a loss of manufacturing competitiveness. One possible factor may have been an overvalued exchange rate. In particular, the period of rapid absolute decline of manufacturing that occurred in the recession of the early 1980s can be linked to the pound's high exchange rate, which resulted from high interest rates and the extremely tight 'monetarist' monetary policy being pursued at the time. Likewise, the recession of the early 1990s led to a further absolute decline of manufacturing, arguably caused by the overvalued rate at which the pound was tied to the ERM between 1990 and 1992.

Other aspects of UK government policy may also have contributed to the relative (and absolute) decline of manufacturing. Broadly, economists divide into two camps or schools of thought. On the one hand are the Keynesians who, together with socialist economists, regard manufacturing decline as a form of market failure caused, for example, by the short-termism of UK financial institutions and the dominance of 'City' financial interests over manufacturing. According to this view, the decline of manufacturing has continued because of too little government intervention to promote long-term investment in manufacturing. But the free-market school of economists, who since 1979 have significantly influenced the Conservative Government in the UK, reject this explanation. In so far as free-market economists see the relative decline of manufacturing as a problem (many of them don't!), they relate the decline to uncompetitiveness caused by too much government intervention rather than too little. They argue that government intervention imposes unnecessary costs on business, for example by creating an inflexible labour market and through the high taxation needed to finance the sheer size of government and the range of activities undertaken by government. According to the free-market view, 'big government' has been the cause of the decline of manufacturing, and competitiveness can be restored only by 'rolling back' the economic functions of the state and getting government 'off the back' of business.

For overall quality of argument: up to 15 marks

Examiner's tip

Sometimes in questions on industrial change, the term 'deindustrialisation' appears explicitly in the wording of the question. On other occasions, as with this question, you are asked to discuss or explain changes in manufacturing alone, and not to consider other sectors (such as coal mining and the railways) that might have experienced decline.

It would be a good idea to start with some figures indicating the relative decline of manufacturing, preferably for selected years since 1979, in order to illustrate any long-term trend and cyclical variations around the trend. In exam conditions, it may be difficult to quote more than an occasional fact or statistic, but try to avoid such debatable generalisations as 'there has been a vast decline in manufacturing'. It is always important to define key terms used in both the question and your answer. At the beginning of your answer, therefore, you should distinguish accurately between a *relative* and an *absolute* decline of manufacturing. Note also the mark allocation. This part of the question carries more than double the marks available for part (b), so you must consider this to get the balance of your answer right.

(b) As the answer to part (a) implies, the various measures which a government could use to reverse the relative decline of manufacturing can be classified as either interventionist or anti-interventionist. Interventionist measures to promote the renewed growth of manufacturing could include the extension of public ownership and the selective directing of state aid to firms which the government hopes will become the industrial success stories of the future. These were tried to some extent by the Labour Government in the 1970s. An extension of public ownership might – in theory at least – both protect industries from structural decline and also allow the government to nurture new areas of manufacturing considered too risky for the private sector.

Not unexpectedly, free-market economists reject all these policies and argue instead that the correct function of government is to be an 'enabler' rather than a 'provider'. In their view, the correct way to deal with the deindustrialisation problem is to 'roll back' state intervention and to create conditions in which private enterprise and entrepreneurial initiative, operating in competitive and efficient markets, can regenerate manufacturing. The state should not attempt to 'pick winners' – such a policy is more likely to end up in 'picking losers'. The free-market approach also argues that as excessive tax rates have in the past created a disincentive to effort, lower tax rates are needed to promote the entrepreneurial flair to ensure the growth of new industries. In its employment policy, the government must make labour markets more competitive and flexible by removing barriers to entry and the monopoly power of trade unions.

Enterprise zones and urban development corporations can be established in areas of economic dereliction. A firm locating in an enterprise zone does not need to obtain planning permission or to make redundancy payments to laid-off workers. They may also benefit from a 'holiday period' extending over several years, during which they pay no local taxation. But critics have argued that enterprise zones seldom attract completely new businesses, and that areas of blight have grown up around enterprise zones as businesses – often warehouses and retail stores rather than manufacturing – have moved into the zones from the surrounding area to benefit from the 'tax holiday'. Urban development corporations such as the London Docklands Urban Development Corporation, are privately sponsored agencies which have been given the authority to attract private development to the previously derelict areas under their control. Like enterprise zones, UDCs are largely outside the political control of the municipalities in which they are located. Free-market

economists believe that because UDCs possess a private enterprise 'culture', they are more effective than government bodies in attracting industry to areas of urban decay.

For each measure listed: up to 5 marks
For development: up to 5 marks each
For overall quality of the discussion: up to 8 marks
Maximum of 30 marks

Examiner's tip

The word 'should' at the beginning of the question is potentially misleading. The question is not asking you to debate the case for and against trying to reverse the relative decline in manufacturing. You must take care to *examine* the measures which could be used. You might conclude by stating which measures you recommend and why, but only after examining a broad spectrum of measures, including those you wish to reject. Base your answer in part upon the actual measures used by UK governments since 1979 to support manufacturing industry.

---

3 (a) (i) The metal manufacturing industry, where employment fell by 53.4% over the period covered by the data. **1 mark**

(ii) The absolute levels of employment for each industry in the first year of the data series, namely 1971, would be required. **2 marks**

Examiner's tip

The first part of the question requires you to identify and state the industry; no elaboration at all is needed. The second part of the question is testing your ability to distinguish between proportionate and absolute changes. You cannot calculate an absolute change from the data in the table unless you know the absolute level of employment in 1971.

(b) (i) Changes in labour productivity (output per worker) over the period shown by the data can be calculated for each industry by subtracting the figure for the % change in output (column 2) from the % change in output. For example, for the first industry group in the table – food, drink and tobacco – the productivity of the labour force rose by over a third, by 34.8%, i.e. output increased by 12% while employment fell by 22.8%. **2 marks**

(ii) Labour productivity increased most of all in electrical engineering by 66.7% (calculated by comparing the 45.3% increase in output and the 21.4% fall in employment. By contrast, labour productivity actually fell in two of the industries in the table: other metal goods and leather goods and fur. In other metal goods, productivity fell by 1.7% (output fell by 32.3% but employment only fell by 30.6%), while for the leather goods and fur industry, productivity fell by 1.8%. **Up to 4 marks**

Examiner's tip

This part of the question is testing your ability to manipulate economic statistics or data. 'Productivity' can be interpreted as labour productivity, which is measured by output per worker. While the data does not show the absolute levels of output and employment for any year, it does show the percentage changes in total output and total employment in each industry. If, for example, total output increases faster than total employment, labour productivity must rise. To answer the second part of the question, you must go through each of the rows of data (except the last one) and subtract the second column from the first column. But take care with the plus and minus figures.

(c) (i) The fact that the table shows that output fell by 21% in the vehicles industry and by 38.3% in the textiles industry, and employment fell by 36% and 50.8% respectively in the two industries, shows that both industries experienced large falls in output and employment over the period 1971 to 1983. However, the falls were greatest in the textile industry. **2 marks**

(ii) The fact that the falls in output and employment were greatest in the textile industry could be explained by a number of contributory factors. These include: the textile industry was less efficient and less able to compete with import competition because over the years textile manufacturers had under-invested in modern capital equipment; the textile industry may have received less financial assistance and protection from the UK government or from the European Community. **4 marks**

Examiner's tip

For the first part of this question, don't just copy out the data for the two industry groups; you must obey the instruction to *compare*. While the question does not ask explicitly for a *contrast*, you should state the main difference in the experience of both industries as shown by the data. This is required for your answer to the second part of the question, where you must go beyond a mere statement and *explain* what you first state.

(d) Deindustrialisation can mean either the relative or absolute decline of manufacturing industry, usually measured in terms of output but possibly also in terms of employment. The data in the table shows the proportional or percentage changes in both output and employment, for manufacturing industries as a whole and also for the different manufacturing industry groupings. Information about the absolute levels of output and employment are needed, together with those for other sectors in the economy, particularly the service sector. Such information would enable a judgment to be made as to whether the decline in output and employment in manufacturing was matched by growth elsewhere in the economy. For example, if a growing service sector took up the 'slack' created by manufacturing decline, the costs of deindustrialisation would be less significant than would be the case if the whole economy were experiencing decline. Other costs of deindustrialisation might relate to the balance of payments, with the decline of manufacturing causing a loss of exports and growing import penetration. Information on manufacturing exports and imports would be useful to assess the significance of this cost.

On the benefit side, the data shows increased labour productivity, indicating possibly that the manufacturing industries which survived the deindustrialisation process were more efficient and competitive, with better prospects for the future. However, other information is needed in order to conclude that manufacturing industry was in better shape in 1983 than it had been in 1971. This could include information on capital investment undertaken by manufacturing firms and details of their profitability. Increased labour productivity might also have resulted in better conditions of work for those employees who kept their jobs. For example robots might have taken over the dull and routine jobs, freeing labour for more fulfilling employment. Information on this, and on wage levels and hours of work, would enable an assessment to be made on whether employment conditions had improved. **For recognition of additional sources of information: up to 3 marks**

For discussion: 2 marks

Examiner's tip

Although the question does not require it, it would be useful to give a brief definition of deindustrialisation. Again, don't just list other useful data or information sources; you must explain how the information would be useful in assessing the costs and benefits of deindustrialisation.

5 PRIVATISATION, REGULATION AND DEREGULATION

Answer **Mark**

1 (a) At the time of their privatisation, businesses such as BT and British Gas were regarded as 'natural' monopolies which couldn't be broken up into smaller competitive companies without a significant loss of economies of scale and productive efficiency. To prevent the newly-privatised utilities from exploiting their monopoly position, for example by restricting services or choice or by hiking up prices, the government set up industry-specific regulatory agencies such as OFTEL and OFWAT. **For relevant background information: up to 3 marks**

The natural monopoly argument: up to 3 marks

The government set up regulatory agencies such as OFGAS and OFWAT for a number of reasons, including the protection of consumers (e.g. gas safety) and 'social' services (e.g. telephone boxes in remote areas). The main reason was to control and reduce the monopoly power of the utility companies, without losing the benefits of economies of scale and dynamic efficiency that large size can allow. The external regulatory bodies act as watchdogs, watching out for and policing monopoly abuse and enforcing good behaviour when such abuse is suspected or discovered. By promoting the removal of any artificial barriers to market entry that protect a monopoly, the regulator may also be able to erode the 'natural' monopoly status of the dominant utility company (rendering it less natural or unnatural!), thereby shifting the market structure towards a more competitive market structure. **Explaining the role of the regulators: up to 7 marks**

Examiner's tip

Whenever privatisation crops up as a term in an examination question, all too many candidates write an answer to a question that hasn't been set, discussing the advantages and disadvantages of privatisation. Remember, however good your answer, you cannot expect to earn any marks if you do not address the set question and adapt your undoubted knowledge to its needs! Also note that this question is about regulation rather than deregulation, though there is some scope for discussion of how a function of the regulatory agencies involves the deregulation of their charges by removing barriers to market entry and by promoting market contestability.

(b) The regulatory agencies have influenced the performance of the industries they oversee in two main ways. Firstly, the regulatory agencies have constrained or limited the commercial freedom of the utility companies to set prices and levels of output as they might choose. Secondly, the agencies have set about removing

artificial barriers protecting the monopoly position of the established firms in order to promote contestability and competition through the entry of new firms. Each of these will be considered in turn. **For promoting easier market entry: up to 3 marks**

The main way in which the regulatory agencies have constrained the freedom of the utility companies to set prices has been through the imposition of a price cap or ceiling based on a formula known as 'RPI minus X'. This is a formula which permits the regulated utility to raise prices each year by an average of the rate of inflation (as measured by the Retail Price Index), minus X per cent fixed by the regulator.

The X factor reflects the improvements in productive efficiency which the regulator believes that the utility can make and share with its consumers each year. The RPI minus X price cap formula is designed to put pressure on the utility to improve productivity and to cut costs. The basic principle is that with X set in the price cap formula for a known period of five years, the utility has the incentive to reduce costs by more than X per cent. In this situation, both the utility and its consumers will benefit from any improvements in productive efficiency. Consumers benefit because real prices – and sometimes also actual prices – fall, and because they know with reasonable certainty the prices they will have to pay. By improving efficiency by more than the 'Factor X' set by the regulator, the utility can benefit from increased profits. The RPI minus X pricing formula thus creates an incentive for British utilities actually to reduce the amount of capital they employ, and to use the subsequently smaller capital stock more efficiently. **Price rules: up to 3 marks**

The regulatory agencies have been able to lower and sometimes remove barriers to market entry by promoting what is called 'technology-driven competition'. This occurs when technical progress enables new firms to enter markets which were previously natural monopolies. In the telecommunications industry, new developments such as satellite technology and the falling real cost of laying fibre-optic land lines that can carry thousands more telephone messages, have meant that new market entrants such as Mercury and the cable television companies can invest in their own distribution networks. BT's distribution network is thus now much less of a 'natural' monopoly.

Of all the utilities, the telecommunication industry offers probably the greatest scope for technology-driven competition, since new technologies such as cable television and cellnet mobile telephones can enable new market entrants to bypass BT's distribution network. But at the other end of the spectrum, the water industry probably possesses the least scope for technology-driven competition to remove barriers to entry and break-up natural monopoly. For this reason, the Office of Water Services has used 'yardstick competition' as the main regulatory device to promote efficient and competitive behaviour by the water companies. After comparing the performance and costs of all the water companies, OFWAT sets prices so that all the water companies have to match the standards achieved by the best in the industry. **Promoting competition: up to 3 marks**

For further relevant discussion: up to 3 marks

Examiner's tip

You could start by stating the assumption that, prior to privatisation, the performance of these industries reflected the state's objectives (e.g. the obligation to provide a 'universal service' at the same price to all customers wherever they lived in the UK), as well as featherbedding and a lack of commercial discipline (due to the fact that the state would write off any loss a nationalised utility might make – though most made large profits for the government). Proceed by arguing that once in the private sector (but unregulated), a utility

company might be expected to indulge in monopoly abuse and to exploit its position by restricting output and choice, and by raising prices so as to make monopoly profit. You could then conclude by explaining – with the use of 'real world' examples – how the regulatory agencies can crack down on monopoly abuse and promote greater competition and efficiency.

---

2 Examiner's answer plan

(a) (i) Explain the background to the question, that whereas industries such as gas, water and telecommunications were privatised whole as vertically-integrated utilities, electricity was sold off as three vertically-disintegrated 'layers': manufacturing or electricity generation – the National Power–PowerGen duopoly; the National Grid company; and the marketing companies such as Yorkshire Electricity, each of which had a monopoly in a particular region. **Up to 10 marks**

(ii) Briefly explain the natural monopoly argument, and how this argument applies to the distribution of the services of utility industries where there is a case for only one power line per street to avoid costly duplication of service. Suggest that on the basis of this argument there is a case for the National Grid and the regional electricity distribution companies being monopolies. **Up to 30 marks**

(iii) Explain that at the time of privatisation an element of competition was introduced into power generation, but only duopolistic competition, together with the potential for some competition from the still state-owned Nuclear Electric. Go on to explain that although power stations may benefit from considerable plant-level economies of scale and possibly firm-level economies of scale in co-ordinating power generation from a number of power stations at peak and off-peak periods, the natural monopoly argument does not apply to power generation. There is therefore a case for removing entry barriers and allowing new power station companies to contest the market. **Up to 40 marks**

(iv) Conclude by discussing whether the track record of the privatised companies indicates that consumers have been exploited, and whether there is a case for more competition in both the production and the distribution layers of the electricity industry. For example, you might introduce evidence of excessive profits made by the regional distributing companies, and of new technology that allows competition without the need for new cables to be laid, thereby getting rid of the natural monopoly argument. **Up to 20 marks**

Examiner's tip

This is rather like two separate questions; you should argue each case separately. Do not debate whether promoting competition in the electricity generation industry is preferable to, or inconsistent with, limiting competition in the distribution of electricity.

---

3 (a) (i) The term 'supply-side strategy' relates to the Conservative Government's overall use of economic policy to improve the competitiveness and efficiency of economic agents (such as workers and entrepreneurs), markets and industries, so that the economy becomes capable of producing more output. The strategy rejects the use of Keynesian demand-management policies; it is microeconomic

rather than macroeconomic; and it is based on promoting free markets while reducing the role of government intervention in the market economy. **2 marks**

(ii) The term 'social benefit' refers to the benefit or gain experienced by the whole community as a result of any action undertaken by individuals, firms or indeed by the government. When, for example, BT invests in a new fibre-optic telecommunication cable in a remote part of Scotland, the extra sales revenue that the cable earns for BT constitutes the private benefit of the investment. However, the social benefit to the whole community is greater, including the benefits to the regional economy which stem from a better communications infrastructure. **2 marks**

Examiner's tip

Make sure you observe the instruction to explain the meaning of the terms *as used in the passage*. You will not be answering the question if you explain a Keynesian or 'interventionist' supply-side strategy. With 'social benefit', you are less likely to be led astray, but stick to explaining benefits rather than social costs. Do not write too much – none of the parts of the question carries more than 4 marks.

(b) Political beliefs lie behind some of the public hostility to privatisation in the UK. In 1979 and during the early 1980s, nearly 40% of the British electorate voted for the Labour Party, which opposed privatisation. Many, though not all, Labour Party voters are socialists who believe that public ownership is both more efficient and more equitable than private ownership. But even amongst non-socialists and believers in the virtues of the free market, there could be an element of hostility to some of the privatisations. Consumers might oppose privatisation of the utility industries, fearing the exercise of producer sovereignty at their expense as the change of ownership replaces public monopoly with private monopoly. Those living in remote areas such as rural Wales might fear lest the privatised utilities withdraw the provision of 'uneconomic' services or introduce much higher prices for customers for whom the cost of providing the service is high. Many people might also believe that the industries were being sold too cheaply and that, as taxpayers and owners of the industries while they were in the public sector, they were not getting a good deal. Finally, a significant minority of the population were actually employed by the nationalised industries. They might fear for their jobs and conditions of work.

Up to 2 marks per reason, maximum of 3 marks

Examiner's tip

The question asks for 'reasons' in the plural, so you must suggest at least two reasons. Public hostility to privatisation may be partly based on people's political views – socialists oppose privatisation. Beware, however, of writing too much of an overtly political nature, either for or against privatisation.

(c) (i) A 'natural monopoly' is said to exist when economies of scale and total market size combine to make it impossible for more than one firm to benefit from full economies of scale. Utility industries such as gas, water and electricity supply, as well as sewage disposal, telecommunications and postal services, are usually cited as the most obvious examples of natural monopolies. **2 marks**

(ii) The utility industries just mentioned have a particular production and marketing problem; they must deliver their service into millions of separate

homes and places of work, usually through a distribution grid of cables or pipelines. High fixed costs of investment in these distribution networks, together with ongoing maintenance costs, mean that there is an obvious case – certainly before recent technological developments – for only one gas pipeline or electricity cable per street, so as to avoid unnecessary duplication. Splitting a national utility into a number of companies, each serving a particular region, does not get over the problem of monopoly; local monopolies simply replace the national monopoly. For competition to be created, new entrants must be allowed into the market. But, as just stated, this could lead to unnecessary duplication, higher average costs and economic waste in the case of natural monopoly. It may also lead to 'cherry picking' or 'cream skimming', whereby the new entrants compete to offer the profitable services but refuse to provide unprofitable 'social' services. If the government does succeed in creating competition in a previously natural monopoly, the resulting market structure is unlikely to resemble perfect competition. It is much more likely to be a case of 'natural oligopoly' replacing natural monopoly.

The answer must relate to natural monopoly to earn all 3 marks

Examiner's tip

While it is a good idea to provide an example of a natural monopoly, an example on its own is not a definition. If you don't understand the meaning of a natural monopoly, you will find it difficult to write a satisfactory answer to the second part of this question.

(d) Privatisation gives a government the immediate benefit of the revenue raised from the sale of a nationalised industry or a state-owned asset such as land. The main long-term benefit which the government seeks is the improvement in efficiency and competitiveness that the transfer of ownership may bring. An increase in competitiveness and efficiency is most likely when, at the time of privatisation, any artificial barriers to market entry or special privileges which protected the state-owned industry are removed. Fear of possible bankruptcy in a private sector environment in which the enterprise's managers and workers know that, in the event of a loss, they will not be baled out by the government, should bring about these benefits. But even if the government sells an industry as an on-going natural monopoly, it may still hope to achieve some of these benefits. Regulatory agencies such as OFWAT and OFFER can act as 'surrogates for competition', simulating the competitive pressures that the government would like to see and seeking ways to remove the barriers to entry that have given the industries their natural monopoly status. Once privatised, the industry faces a form of commercial pressure to improve efficiency which does not affect nationalised business enterprises – the threat of a hostile takeover bid. Last but not least, in the case of the British privatisations, the Conservative Government has hoped to gain the political benefit of a shareholding electorate which now has a financial interest in the health of the privatised industries, and therefore continues to return the Conservative Party to office.

Up to 2 marks per benefit, maximum of 4 marks

Examiner's tip

This question is also worded in the plural. When answering this type of question, you might work on the assumption that two benefits explained in depth, or four or more benefits listed and briefly explained, are needed for full marks to be earned.

(e) Two alternatives to privatisation will be described in this answer. These are: the 'contracting out' of the provision of public sector services to private sector firms and 'competitive tendering'. Contracting out or contractualisation is closely related to privatisation, and indeed is sometimes included in the definition of privatisation. It occurs when services which were previously produced 'in-house' by public sector workers are supplied instead by outside firms which function as subcontractors. Examples include hospital and school catering and cleaning, the emptying of dustbins on behalf of local authorities by private contractors, and the running of prisons by firms such as Group-4 Security. Contractualisation does not usually increase consumer choice, since the service continues to be supplied as a monopoly. However, when combined with competitive tendering, contractualisation does introduce competition into the actual production or delivery of the service. Competitive tendering means that the contract to supply a service to a nationalised industry or a government department is put out to tender. In principle, the outside supplier that can offer the best service at the lowest cost should win the contract. It may also be possible for an in-house team of managers and workers to head off all outside bids and win the contract. The 'internal market' recently introduced in the National Health Service involves a variant of competitive tendering. Fund-holding local doctors or GPs 'shop around', buying surgical services for their patients from the hospitals or 'providers' who can deliver the required service at the lowest cost to the doctor's budget.

Up to 2 marks per measure, maximum of 4 marks

Examiner's tip

Make sure you follow the instruction to discuss *fully* the various options. This means you should write at least three or four sentences on each of the alternatives you cover in your answer. Note that the policies you describe should not be regarded simply as alternatives to privatisation – supporters of privatisation regard them as complementary policies in a wider policy of economic liberalisation.

6 MARKET FAILURE

Answer	Mark

1 (a) Pure public goods are defined by the twin characteristics of non-excludability and non-diminishability, but it is the latter which is most relevant to this question. The non-diminishability of a pure public good such as national defence means that an extra person can consume and benefit from the good without reducing the quantity available for other people. Consumption does not need to be rationed, even when the good is provided at zero price. Scarce resources are nevertheless used up in the provision of the public good, so the government (which is usually the provider) still has to decide how much tax revenue and physical resources to devote to the good's provision. 'Production rationing' rather than 'consumption rationing' therefore takes place. With a 'non-pure' or 'quasi' public good such as a road, matters are more

complicated. While the road is more or less empty or unused, there is no need to ration road use, but as soon as congestion occurs, a rationing problem does arise.

For defining and distinguishing between public and private goods: up to 4 marks
For explaining that consumption of public goods need not be rationed: up to 4 marks
For discussing the meaning of rationing: up to 3 marks

A private good is simply a good which isn't a public good; it has the properties of excludability (the owner can exclude others from consuming and receiving its benefits), and diminishability (consumption by one person reduces the quantity available for others). It is the latter property which creates the need for consumption rationing as well as production rationing in the case of private goods. This rationing is of course usually performed by the price mechanism.

For explaining that prices ration the consumption of private goods: up to 4 marks

Examiner's tip

A private good is simply the opposite of a public good. Probably all your personal possessions such as a CD player or a pair of designer boots are private goods; you can exercise 'private property rights' and prevent other people from using them – unless of course you rent them out or simply let your friends use them! And, because they possess the twin characteristics of excludability and diminishability which define a private good, merit goods provided by the state, such as health care and education, are also private goods rather than public goods.

(b) (i) Merit goods provided by governments, such as education and health care, are also private goods, and must not be confused with public goods. With these goods, shortages will occur if they are made available at zero price, unless of course the government commits a super-abundance of resources to their provision. Free provision of merit goods by the government therefore requires some form of rationing to deal with the excess demand which occurs when the good is provided free. For popular university courses, queues and waiting lists provide a crude method of quantity rationing. Students are sometimes told to wait a year before they can be admitted to a popular course. Queues and waiting lists are not, however, the main methods of rationing used to limit entry to higher education. For the most part, universities use minimum entry requirements such as specified A-level grades for this purpose, raising the grades required as a course becomes more popular.

For rationing by qualification: up to 5 marks

(ii) And while queues and waiting lists have certainly been the main method of rationing NHS hospital beds, other rationing devices have been used, such as doctors' assessments of 'degree of need', and also the price mechanism when patients opt for a private bed to by-pass the waiting list.

Current NHS reforms being introduced by the Conservative Government are also relevant to the question. Under the reforms, the NHS is still being funded by the taxpayer and available (for the most part) at zero price to the consumer, but an 'internal market' has been introduced within the health service which functions as a 'surrogate' price mechanism. Family doctors or GPs who have opted into the reformed system are allocated budgets by the NHS administrators. The doctors then spend these budgets by buying hospital services for their patients, making decisions on the basis of degree of need and by shopping around for the hospitals that offer the service at the best price. Prices paid by the patient are now used to ration NHS dentistry services, and

it is quite likely that as a part of a future 'reform', patients will be charged for services such as bed linen and meals received in NHS hospitals.

Queues and waiting lists: up to 3 marks
Price mechanism and internal market: up to 2 marks

Examiner's tip

There is a possible danger here of confusing a good which happens to be free with a genuine free good. The air you breathe is a free good, because it is available in unlimited quantities at zero cost of production. For a free good, there is no problem of scarcity, and hence no need to use the price mechanism or any other allocative device, such as the state command mechanism, to ration either production or consumption of the good. By contrast, all of us consume many goods for 'free' – in the sense that we are not charged a price in order to benefit from them. These goods – such as defence, police, education and health services – are provided for public good or merit good reasons. Because scarce resources are used up in their production, resource usage still has to be rationed. And in the case of merit goods, excess demand exists at the zero or subsidised price at which they are provided by the state; therefore consumption has also to be rationed.

---

2 Until a few years ago, it was usual for UK governments to intervene in the free market economy in order to reduce inequalities in the distribution of income. To achieve this objective, they used progressive taxation – under which higher income groups pay a larger proportion of their income to the government than lower income groups – and transfers in the form of welfare benefits.

Before 1979, the main effect was to create a more equal distribution of income and wealth than that brought about by market forces alone. The main effect of the policies implemented since 1979 has been the complete reverse. Inequalities in the distribution of income and wealth have widened rather than narrowed.

Outline of effects before and after 1979: up to 8 marks

It is important to understand that supply-side economists believe that policies pursued before 1979 (which reduced inequalities) also had a most significant unintended effect. In the supply-side view, they destroyed personal incentives, made the economy uncompetitive and slowed the economy's growth rate. Indeed, for supply-siders, they provided a prime example of government failure. The supply-siders believe that policies pursued since 1979 have had the reverse effect – the creation of an efficient, competitive enterprise economy, marked by greater personal incentives, greatly reduced evasion and avoidance, and the elimination of a dependency culture.

Free-market supply-side economists argued that to make everyone – including the poor – ultimately better off, the poor must first be made worse off! They believed increased inequalities were necessary to produce the conditions in which a growing 'economic cake' could allow everyone to be better off in absolute terms in the long run, though even if the policy were successful, the poor would remain relatively worse off compared to the rich. Opponents argued that to use tax and benefits policies to widen income inequalities was unethical and was not justified by any improvement in the economy's performance. Keynesians argued that the policy was based on a false premise – that to create the incentives deemed necessary to make the economy perform better, the already wealthy had to be offered even more wealth, while the already poor were threatened with even greater poverty.

For further development: up to 12 marks

Examiner's tip

You are probably very familiar with questions on market failure. This is an example of a new type of question on government failure rather than market failure. Government failure occurs when, in trying to correct market failure, government intervention either makes matters worse or creates completely new problems, distortions or inefficiencies. You should go beyond a narrow discussion of how progressive taxation and welfare benefits paid to the poor might reduce income inequalities. The question is looking for something a little bit extra in order to earn a really high pass mark, namely the free-market supply-side argument. Fashionable during the Thatcherite years of the 1980s, this argument contended that a greater inequality in the distribution of income was needed to create the personal incentives necessary for a faster rate of economic growth.

---

3 (a) Acid rain is an example of a negative externality, discharged into the atmosphere as a by-product when coal is burnt to produce electricity. When a power station burns coal, it only considers the cost of the fuel and other factors of production. Pollution costs are not included in the price charged to households and industrial users for the electricity they consume. As a result, electricity is underpriced, encouraging too much consumption and hence too many of society's scarce resources are being allocated to this particular usage. **Pollution as an externality: up to 2 marks**
Why this is a market failure: up to 2 marks

Examiner's tip

The danger with this type of question is that you will write too much about market failure in general and not enough about pollution as a negative externality, and why a negative externality leads to a market failure. Make sure you stick to the economics and resist the temptation to veer into writing a 'green' answer devoted to lengthy but irrelevant description of how acid rain pollution corrodes buildings and kills plant life and fish.

(b) (i) 'Regulatory-driven market' is a reference to the way the electricity market is run. Although electricity production is undertaken by private enterprise, government-appointed agencies (the Environmental Protection Agency in the context of the American example in the passage, and the Office of Electricity Regulation in the UK) regulate or impose constraints on the freedom of power stations to pollute (in the American example) or to raise prices (in the case of OFFER in the UK).
Market regulated or constrained by a regulator: up to 3 marks

(ii) By trading excess pollution allowances, companies that reduce pollution by more than is required will be able to generate extra income or revenue. The benefit may then be passed on, partly or whole, to consumers in the form of lower electricity bills. **One benefit only required: up to 3 marks**

Examiner's tip

Both parts of this question test comprehension of material in the passage. You should be able to work out that a 'regulatory-driven' market is one where some form of regulation, either government imposed or industry 'self-regulation', limits the freedom of firms to set prices or levels of output. Part (ii) requires discussion of how consumers may benefit from lower prices rather than a wider-ranging discussion of environmental benefits or benefits to shareholders.

(c) The passage identifies three ways in which demand or supply curves may shift between Phases 1 and 2, thereby causing the price of pollution permits to rise from \$250–\$300 to about \$600. In Phase 1, the demand curve for permits is D_1 and the supply curve of permits is S_1, as in the diagram below.

Firstly, and perhaps most importantly, the demand curve for permits is expected to shift rightwards from D_1 to D_2, because the demand for electricity is expected to rise. This illustrates 'derived demand'; in order to be able to produce more electricity to meet consumer demand, the power stations will need more permits to enable them to discharge legally the extra pollution that the extra production of electricity necessitates.

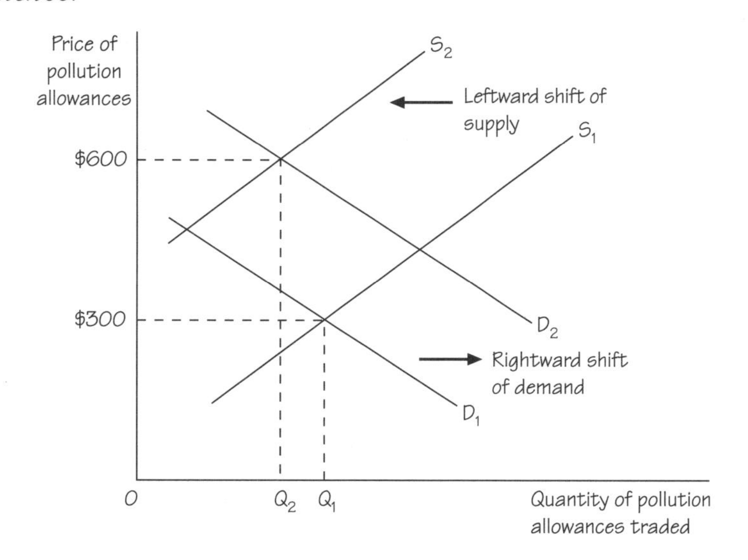

Secondly, this rightward shift of the demand curve for permits from D_1 to D_2 is likely to be reinforced because firms will be unable to meet the annual reduction in allowable pollution simply by installing new technology. This leads to the third factor contributing to the rise in the price of permits: the supply curve of permits may shift leftwards from S_1 to S_2 because as fewer power stations over-comply, there are fewer 'spare' allowances available. More power stations will become buyers rather than suppliers of pollution permits.

For each method identified and explained: up to 3 marks, maximum of 6 marks

Examiner's tip

In examination conditions, candidates all too often perform poorly when asked to apply supply and demand analysis to illustrate textual data. With this question, the dangers are: (i) drawing a supply and demand diagram without indicating whether it represents a market for pollution permits or the market for electricity itself; (ii) leaving axes of diagrams unlabelled; (iii) wrongly labelling a demand curve as a supply curve and vice versa; and (iv) confusing a movement along a curve and a shift of the curve.

The key instruction here is: 'With the aid of supply and demand analysis, explain . . .'. This means that supply and demand diagrams are not essential – provided that you undertake relevant supply and demand analysis in a written account. Having said this, it is much more straightforward to use at least one supply and demand diagram to illustrate the main points that need to be made.

(d) (i) Sulphur dioxide pollution may also be limited by the imposition of a pollution tax upon the offending companies. The tax should be proportional to the quantity of pollution discharged so that, under the 'polluter must pay' principle, an incentive is created, which is otherwise lacking in the market, for less pollution

to be emitted. In principle, this will close the divergence between the private and the social cost of producing electricity, thereby leading to a socially optimal outcome.
For stating method: 1 mark
For elaboration: 1 mark

(ii) Along with a pollution tax scheme, the market in pollution permits described in the passage has the advantage of working with the market rather than against it, in the sense that it creates financial incentives for polluters to alter their levels and methods of production in a more socially desirable way. The system may also be fairly cheap to operate. As with other methods of trying to reduce pollution, the permits system has, however, the disadvantage that companies may cheat by trying to avoid detection when they discharge pollution into the atmosphere. It also increases the total amount of regulation and interference in private industry, which is considered a disadvantage by free-market economists. Blanket prohibition of pollution might, of course, be the most effective way of reducing the total quantity of pollutants emitted into the atmosphere, but it has the obvious danger of 'throwing the baby out with the bath water', in the sense that consumer welfare would undoubtedly suffer if it was no longer possible to produce the 'good' electricity once the 'bad' pollution had been completely banned.
For stating advantage or disadvantage: up to 2 marks each
Discussion: up to 3 marks
Maximum of 7 marks

Examiner's tip

To gain marks with part (i), you have to introduce a method of limiting sulphur dioxide pollution which is independent of the market in 'permits to pollute'. It is not enough just to mention fines or the imposition of maximum limits or ceilings on pollution. Without further elaboration or qualification, neither of these can earn any credit since they are described in the passage as part of the 'permits to pollute' scheme. Also, you must briefly explain how the method you mention will work. With part (ii) the danger is that you will ignore the word 'methods' and just consider the pros and cons of controlling pollution. It would be very easy to write a careless answer as a result of not spending enough time reading the precise wording of the question.

7 THE LABOUR MARKET AND EMPLOYMENT ISSUES

Answer **Mark**

1 The most obvious explanation suggested by conventional market theory for differences in wage levels is that the labour demand and supply curves are in different positions in different labour markets, reflecting such factors as different labour productivities, abilities and required skills. Secondly, real life labour markets are imperfectly competitive, characterised by imperfect market information and by barriers and sources of friction which prevent or restrict movement between markets. Thirdly, the theory of wage discrimination may operate in imperfectly competitive labour markets, allowing employers to pay their workers different wages equal to each worker's transfer earnings (the minimum wage required for each worker to be prepared to supply labour). According

to this theory, many women workers are prepared to work for lower wages than men; therefore they are paid less! **For introductory listing of causes: up to 6 marks**

Even within the rarefied and abstract assumptions of perfect competition, we might expect certain wage differentials to exist at any point in time. This is for two main reasons. Firstly, different jobs have different non-monetary characteristics. The 'net advantage' of any type of work includes job satisfaction or dissatisfaction as well as the utility of the wage. Other things being equal, a worker must be paid a higher wage to compensate for any relative unpleasantness in the job. An 'equalising wage differential' is the payment which must be made to compensate a worker for the different non-monetary characteristics of jobs so that following the payment, the worker has no incentive to switch between jobs or labour markets. Secondly, at any point in time, the labour market is unlikely to be in equilibrium, in which case disequilibrium trading takes place. **For disequilibrium trading and non-monetary factors: up to 3 marks**

Some economists argue that conventional distribution theory and marginal productivity theory fail to take account of the role of institutional and social factors in determining wages and other factor incomes. They argue that the role of power conferred on different groups through the political and legal system is the main institutional factor responsible for determining incomes, both between different groups of workers and also between pay and profits. Relevant social factors which influence wage determination include conventional attitudes within society to differentials between the wages received by different groups of workers, skilled and unskilled, young and old, male and female, etc. **For institutional and social factors: up to 3 marks**

In recent years, the growth in the labour force by 3.8 million has been almost entirely due to women taking on jobs. However, in 1991, female average hourly earnings were £5.89 per hour compared to £7.57 for males, and women were 2.75 times more likely than men to be earning less than £3.40 per hour. There are two main reasons why women earn less than men. Firstly, women work predominantly in low-paid industries and occupations. Secondly, within many occupational groups, women are often paid less than men, because they are under-represented in the higher-paid posts within an occupation, rather than because they are paid less for doing the same job.

For reasons: up to 2 marks each

Wage discrimination against women (which was mentioned in the introductory paragraph to this answer), may of course contribute to both these sets of circumstances. In addition, women are disproportionately represented in industries where the average size of firm and plant is small. These industries tend to pay lower wages and offer fewer promotional prospects than large firms and large industries. Also, these industries are seldom unionised. Indeed, within all industries, women workers are less unionised than men. This relates to another reason why women earn less than men; on average, their attachment to the labour force is weaker. Each year of work experience raises the pay of both men and women by an average 3 per cent. Yet when women leave the labour force, usually to look after young children, their potential pay falls by 3 per cent for each year involved. If, for example, a man and woman enter employment with equal potential and after 8 years the woman leaves the work force for a further 8 years in order to raise a family, she may re-enter the labour force 16 years behind the man in pay terms. The higher labour turnover of women also imposes costs on the employer, such as the cost of training replacement workers. This may reduce the incentive for employers to train female workers. Similarly, women may have less incentive to spend time and money on their own education and training if they expect the benefits they will eventually receive will be less than the costs initially incurred.

For wage discrimination: up to 5 marks

To what extent therefore does conventional economic theory satisfactorily account for the pattern of employment and pay, both in general terms and more specifically in terms of the differences between male and female pay? I shall conclude by arguing that the marginal productivity or market approach and the social and institutional approach to wage determination are not necessarily incompatible. Social and institutional factors are important determinants of the conditions of supply and demand in individual labour market, of the conditions of supply of male and female workers, and of the barriers which separate labour markets and contribute to market imperfection. For example, if a group of workers wants to raise its wages above the equilibrium level determined by supply and demand, it may only be able to do so in the long run by taking steps to influence the demand and supply schedules for the type of labour involved, e.g. by restrictive practices to limit the flow of new entrants, or in the case of state employees such as nurses, by persuading the government to employ more nurses, thereby shifting the demand curve for nurses to the right. **For conclusions: up to 4 marks**

Maximum of 25 marks

Examiner's tip

This is an example of an 'unstructured' essay question, i.e. a question which has not been divided into parts, each with a separate mark allocation. The fact that the mark allocation has not been shown means that you must use your judgment when deciding how much time to devote to each part of the question. You could start your answer by mentioning at least two, and preferably more, possible causes of wage differentials, before going on to explain each cause in greater depth. Make sure you explain clearly how wages may reflect different marginal productivities, but also allot some space to cultural and institutional factors. You might start your answer to the second part of the question by discussing whether economic theory adequately explains wage differentials between different types of jobs and skills. Then outline how the theory of wage discrimination might explain lower wages paid to women for doing the same job as men. Conclude your answer by discussing whether this is a sufficient explanation of the generally lower wages paid to women.

---

2 (a) There are two ways of explaining the meaning of the natural rate of unemployment. The first method defines the natural rate in relation to the aggregate labour market, whereas the second method makes use of 'Phillips curve' analysis and the concept of the 'expectations-augmented Phillips curve'. In the former approach, the economy's equilibrium level of employment (the natural level of employment) is determined at the market-clearing real wage at which employers' aggregate demand for labour equals the aggregate supply of labour of the economy's labour force.

For introducing the concept of the natural rate: up to 8 marks

The difference between the economy's natural or equilibrium level of employment and the amount of labour available in the economy then constitutes the natural *level* of unemployment. The natural *rate* of unemployment is the natural level of unemployment as a percentage of the available labour force. The natural rate of unemployment is made up of frictional unemployment and (according to some authorities) structural unemployment. Both these types of unemployment result from processes of dynamic change in the economy. Frictional unemployment occurs because workers voluntarily choose to remain unemployed 'between jobs', even though vacancies exist which, in principle, they could fill. Structural unemployment is more deep-seated. Workers become structurally unemployed when the industries enter structural decline or shed labour when they adopt new technologies.

For explaining the natural rate: up to 12 marks

The diagram below shows the natural rate of unemployment on a Phillips curve. The vertical line PC_L is the long-run Phillips curve which locates the natural rate of unemployment. To answer part (b) of this question, this diagram will be used to explain the effect on the economy of an expansion of demand which reduces unemployment below the natural rate (and to the left of the long-run Phillips curve).

For illustration on a Phillips curve diagram: up to 10 marks

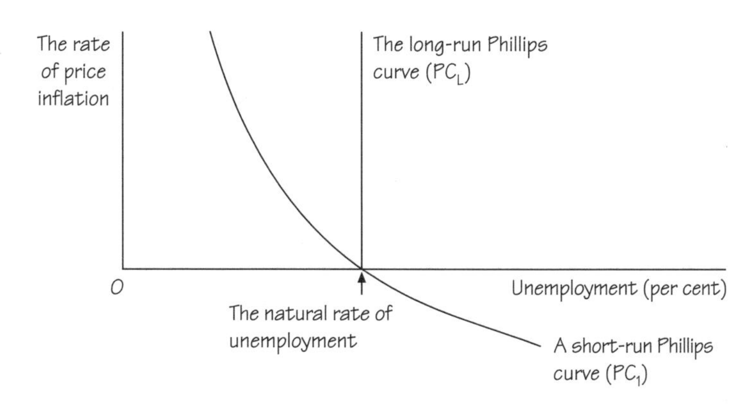

Examiner's tip

Start your answer with a definition of the natural rate of unemployment, preferably illustrating your answer with a diagram showing either the aggregate labour market or the 'expectations-augmented Phillips curve'. Explain how the natural rate of unemployment is made up of frictional and possibly structural unemployment, but make sure you don't rewrite the question as 'write all you know about frictional and structural unemployment'.

(b) Even amongst those economists who believe that there is a natural rate of unemployment, there is considerable disagreement on its size. In early 1995, the consensus view seemed to be that for the UK, the natural rate was around 8 to 8.5 per cent of the labour force, a figure just below the then unemployment rate of 8.8 per cent. The level of unemployment at the natural rate would have been around 2,400,000. Professor Patrick Minford, however, believed that because of the success of the Conservative Government's supply-side reforms, the UK's natural rate of unemployment had fallen back to a level last sustained in the 1950s, at around 2.5 per cent of the labour force, or 600,000 unemployed.

For discussing the size of the natural rate: up to 6 marks

If Professor Minford's view is correct, then the government could use demand-side policies to expand demand so as to reduce unemployment towards its natural rate without destabilising the economy. However, if the consensus view is correct, demand-side policies must be rejected because the economy is already too close to its natural rates of output and employment.

There is general agreement amongst monetarist and free-market economists – including Professor Minford – that any attempt to use demand-side policies to reduce unemployment *below* its natural rate (wherever that may be) will be ineffective in the long run. They believe that unless quickly reversed, such a policy will destabilise the economy and eventually cause the natural rate to increase.

To explain this, I will return to the Phillips curve diagram included in the answer to part (a). When the government expands demand to reduce unemployment below the natural rate, it trades-off along the short-run Phillips curve PC_1, accepting the fact that the inflation rate will rise as unemployment falls. But one of the factors fixing

the position of the short-run Phillips curve PC_1 is the expected rate of inflation. As unemployment falls below the natural rate, the actual rate of inflation begins to exceed the expected rate. Phillips curve PC_1 no longer remains operational – and the short-run Phillips curve shifts upwards. As workers and firms come to realise that inflation is higher than the rate they were expecting, they refuse to supply the labour and produce the output necessary for unemployment to be sustained below, and for output to be sustained above, their natural levels.

If the government realises its mistake and refuses to finance any further increase in the inflation rate, output and unemployment will return to their natural levels, with the inflation rate stabilising at the rate brought about by the initial trade-off along PC_1. The economy returns to the long-run Phillips curve, but at a higher rate of inflation than before the expansion of demand reduced unemployment (temporarily) below its natural level. If the government is foolish enough to finance an ever-accelerating rate of inflation, unemployment can only be sustained below its natural rate for a time. Eventually, as inflation accelerates towards hyper-inflation, the rate of inflation will damage the economy to such an extent that not only will it be impossible to continue to keep unemployment below its natural rate, but the natural rate of unemployment will also increase.

For discussing the effectiveness of demand-side policies: up to 32 marks

In the free-market view, the appropriate supply-side policies to reduce the natural rate of unemployment include: tax cuts to create incentives to work, save and invest; cuts in welfare benefits to create an incentive to choose work rather than unemployment, together with labour market reforms which reduce the power of trade unions; and the pro-market industrial policies of privatisation, marketisation and deregulation. As already noted, Professor Patrick Minford believes that the implementation of these supply-side policies has already been successful in significantly reducing the natural rate of unemployment in the UK, but other commentators are not so optimistic. Many economists believe that while such supply-side reforms are indeed necessary to restore and maintain the competitiveness of the UK economy, the natural rate will nevertheless remain much higher for the foreseeable future than it was a generation ago. Most of the explanation lies in the growth of structural and technological unemployment. Despite the supply-side reforms, the shift of manufacturing to the 'tiger' economies of newly industrialising countries (NICs) such as South Korea and Taiwan, may mean that UK manufacturing employment can never recover to the level which preceded the deindustrialisation of the 1970s and 1980s. At the same time, the spread of automation and the impact of information technology in the more successful parts of the UK economy have often led to labour-shedding and redundancy rather than to an overall increase in employment.

For discussing the effectiveness of supply-side policies: up to 32 marks

Examiner's tip

The key word here is *evaluate*. This means that you must go further than simply describing demand-side and supply-side economic policies and how they operate. You must assess the appropriateness of both types of policy, both for reducing unemployment towards the natural rate, and also for reducing the natural rate of unemployment itself.

3 Keynesian economic policies are those policies advocated by members of the Keynesian school of economists, who support the theories and economic approach formulated by the great economist, J M Keynes, in the 1920s and 1930s. Keynes located a major cause of unemployment on the demand side of the economy, believing that excessive saving and too little spending of income were major contributors to unemployment.

For explaining the term 'Keynesian': up to 2 marks

In recent years, the term 'supply-side economics' has been coined to describe the theories of the anti-Keynesian school of economists, many of whom are also known as monetarists, neoclassical or 'free-market' economists. For the most part, supply-side economists reject the Keynesian argument that demand-deficiency is an important cause of unemployment, though they do accept that it can temporarily occur (as cyclical unemployment) in the downswing of the business cycle. They believe, however, that provided the economy is sufficiently competitive, market forces will automatically reduce this type of unemployment, largely through a fall in the rate of interest which will stimulate consumption and investment and eliminate excess savings.

For explaining the term 'supply-side': up to 2 marks

Keynesian economists see unemployment, along with most other economic problems, as a problem of market failure, resulting from the inefficient functioning of the market economy. They believe that through a policy of active intervention, the government can correct the market failure and eliminate demand-deficient unemployment.

For outlining the Keynesian view: up to 2 marks

Supply-side economists generally take the completely opposite view. For them, large-scale unemployment is a problem of government failure rather than market failure. Unemployment was created by decades of government interference in the economy (from the 1940s through to the 1970s). Government intervention destroyed incentives for workers to supply labour and for entrepreneurs to create jobs and demand the services of labour. As a result, markets functioned inefficiently and the natural levels of output and employment have been lower (and the natural level of unemployment higher) than they would have been if governments had always pursued pro-market supply-side policies rather than interventionist Keynesian policies.

For outlining the supply-side view: up to 2 marks

If, as Keynesians have traditionally believed, unemployment is caused by excessive saving and by deficient demand, it follows that the correct policy solution is to inject just enough demand back into the economy to counter the leakage of demand through saving. Suppose now that within the private sector, household saving exceeds the investment by firms: ($S > I$). Keynesians argue that in these circumstances an attempt by the government to balance its budget (i.e. to set $G = T$) will create deficient demand in the economy, unless of course the excess savings of the households were matched by an excess of export demand over imports in the overseas sector. Keynesians argue that when saving by households exceeds the investment spending of firms, the government should deliberately deficit finance, running a budget deficit ($G > T$) exactly equal to the excess of saving over investment. Via the public sector borrowing requirement (PSBR), with which the government sector's budget deficit is financed, the government borrows the excess savings of the private sector, which it spends itself, thereby injecting demand back into the economy and preventing the emergence of deficient demand.

For Keynesian policy solutions: up to 5 marks

By contrast, many supply-side economists believe that governments should aim for the 'financial orthodoxy' or 'sound finance' of a balanced budget. Some supply-side economists accept that a deficit is permissible as a method of reducing unemployment during a recession, but that the government should aim to balance its budget over the

whole of a business cycle. During a recession, a budget deficit functions as an automatic stabiliser. The deficit reduces the extent to which demand falls in the economy, and dampens or stabilises the downturn.

According to the supply-side view, Keynesians wish to reduce unemployment *below* its natural rate by expanding demand. They argue that this is irresponsible and ultimately ineffective. Although it may be possible to use Keynesian policies to reduce unemployment below the natural rate in the short run (at the expense of inflation), the reduction cannot be sustained. Supply-siders believe that the only correct and sustainable way to reduce unemployment is by reducing the natural rate itself.

The labour market measures which supply-side economists believe are necessary to create the conditions in which the natural rate of unemployment can fall include: income tax reductions to create labour market incentives; reducing state welfare benefits – incentives to choose low-paid employment rather than unemployment, and to reduce the 'unemployment trap'; removing protection for workers in low-paid industries (such as Wages Councils) and resisting calls for the introduction of minimum wage legislation and for compliance with the EU Social Chapter; reducing the powers of trade unions by removing legal protection from trade unions, restricting their rights, and extending the freedom for workers not to belong to unions and for employers not to recognise and negotiate with unions; replacing collective bargaining with individual wage negotiation and by employer determination of pay; restricting the right to strike and to undertake industrial action. **For supply-side policy solutions: up to 5 marks**

To some extent this debate between Keynesians and supply-side economists has been overtaken by events. It is now widely agreed, by Keynesians as well as by supporters of the free market, that the cause of most modern unemployment in countries such as the UK lies on the supply side of the economy – rather than on the demand side. There is much disagreement, however, on the appropriate policies to improve supply-side performance so as to achieve a significant reduction in unemployment. Thus the supply-side policies thought appropriate by Keynesians differ significantly from the free-market policies described so far. Keynesian supply-side policy would once again extend the economic role of the state through an active microeconomic policy of financial assistance to industry.

For overall comparison: up to 7 marks

Examiner's tip

In order to compare the policies, you must first give a brief account of the different Keynesian and supply-side theories of the causes of unemployment. Then describe the policies which economists of the two schools believe appropriate for reducing unemployment, making sure that you indicate how the policies are supposed to work. Conclude by assessing the effectiveness of the policies, perhaps rounding off your answer by stating which school you support and why.

8 MACROECONOMIC POLICY

Answer	Mark

1 (a) It is usual to think of the government's economic policy objectives as being macroeconomic rather than microeconomic. With this in mind, four macroeconomic objectives are commonly identified. These are: full employment; economic growth; price stability or control of inflation; and an external objective relating to the balance of payments and the exchange rate, though the exact nature of this objective depends on the type of exchange rate (floating or fixed) which is in place. Governments may sometimes also wish to achieve a fairer or more equitable distribution of income and wealth. This 'distributional' objective can be regarded as being more microeconomic than macroeconomic.

For listing objectives: up to 3 marks

In recent years, full employment has been defined in terms of the natural rate of unemployment, i.e. the rate of unemployment which is consistent with a stable inflation rate. This definition of full employment accepts that there is still some frictional and structural unemployment even when the economy is 'fully employed'. The natural rate has also been called the 'full employment rate of unemployment'. Economic growth involves increasing the economy's production potential and the outward movement of the economy's production possibility frontier so as to increase real output per head and economic welfare.

Some economists believe that the objective of controlling inflation should mean the pursuit of complete price stability, i.e. zero inflation. Others argue that the costs of complete price stability – in terms of loss of output, employment and welfare – would exceed the benefits. They believe that governments should aim for a low and non-accelerating rate of inflation. As noted, the government's external policy objective depends on the exchange rate system. In a floating exchange rate regime, the objective may be to allow the exchange rate to rise or fall to whatever level is consistent with balance of payments equilibrium. By contrast, in a fixed system the external objective may be to support the fixed exchange rate by fighting pressures that might otherwise force its devaluation or revaluation.

Finally, it is worth noting that the *ultimate* objective of any government (besides pursuing the goal of remaining in power!) is to improve the general level of economic welfare enjoyed by the population. If this is the case, then all policies, macroeconomic and microeconomic, are undertaken with this underlying objective in mind.

For relevant development: up to 3 marks

Examiner's tip

You must make a judgment on how to interpret the word 'recent'. With data questions, the examining boards expect you to be familiar with the UK economy over the ten years or so before the examination, so it would be in order to draw on the experience of the last ten years. Alternatively you could go back to 1979, when monetarist and supply-side macro policy replaced the Keynesianism which had dominated the previous quarter-century. Your answer need not be restricted to macroeconomics; the wording of the question gives scope for describing microeconomic objectives as well. It is worth making the point that to a significant extent, in recent years supply-side economic policy has been predominantly microeconomic rather than macroeconomic.

(b) The main measures a government can use to achieve its various policy objectives can be grouped under the headings of 'monetary policy' instruments, 'fiscal policy' instruments and 'direct controls'. The measures a government actually chooses to implement depend to a large extent on the government's views on how the economy works. In the past, Keynesian-inspired governments used fiscal policy as the main policy instrument to manage demand to try to achieve full employment, economic growth and control of inflation. They also used direct controls such as incomes policy to control inflation, and controls on bank lending (in monetary policy) to supplement fiscal policy in the management of demand. Some Keynesians have recommended another type of direct control, import controls, to deal with a balance of payments deficit. **For a basic statement of measures: up to 6 marks**

All of these are rejected by monetarist and supply-side economists. Believing in the virtues of the free market, they consider interventionist measures such as incomes policy to be completely inappropriate, creating inefficiencies and distortions in the economy and in any case ineffective. And although free-market economists advocate the use of monetary and fiscal policy to achieve desired policy objectives, they do not believe that policy should be based on the management of aggregate demand.

Monetarists believe that at the heart of economic policy, a tight monetary policy should be used to control inflation. This could be based on a 'monetary policy rule'. The government would publish a target rate of growth for the money supply and announce that it would implement monetary policy so as to 'hit' the money supply target. Such a policy was tried in the early 1980s in the UK, but it did not work very well. As a result, many monetarists believed that the control of inflation should be based on the exchange rate as the principal monetary policy instrument. A high exchange rate might reduce inflation in a number of ways. Firstly and most directly, it reduces the prices of imported food, energy, raw materials and consumer goods. Secondly and less directly, a high exchange rate creates an incentive for workers and firms within the domestic economy to negotiate wages and set prices in a less inflationary way, lest they destroy international trading competitiveness and price themselves out of jobs and markets.

This policy was also tried from 1990 to 1992, when the pound was fixed within the ERM, but again the policy could not be sustained. Since the exit from the ERM, a 'pre-emptive strike' strategy has formed the main plank of the government's counter-inflation policy. The monetary authorities publish an inflation target and announce that, if necessary, interest rates will be raised even when there is no obvious sign that inflation is accelerating, to pre-empt or 'nip in the bud' inflation that would otherwise arise several months ahead. As yet, there is insufficient evidence to show whether a 'pre-emptive strike'-based monetary policy is the most appropriate measure to control inflation.

Monetarist and supply-side economists believe that with respect to full employment and economic growth, government should be an *enabler* rather than a *provider*. They believe that interventionist macro policies cannot create jobs and that the function of government is to create the conditions in which millions of individuals pursuing their self-interest bring about improvements in economic welfare. While monetary policy should be used to create price stability, appropriate pro-market supply-side policies should be used to create the other necessary conditions, namely a low-tax environment and competitive and efficient markets.

For explaining each measure: up to a further 3 marks each, maximum of 8 marks

Examiner's tip

Whereas part (a) of this question is concerned with policy *objectives*, part (b) requires you to show a knowledge of the policy *instruments* which a government might use to try to achieve the objectives described in your answer. The key words in the question are 'full account' and 'can'. You must go beyond a mere definition of policy types (such as monetary policy and fiscal policy), and give some indication of how each might be used to achieve one or more policy objectives. The word 'can' means that you don't have to restrict your answer to past experience; if you so wish you might discuss how a policy measure could be expected to work in principle. It is probably easier to draw on UK experience of actual policy measures which recent governments have implemented.

(c) If all the government's economic policy objectives could be achieved simultaneously, the 'economic problem' would largely disappear! But it is difficult if not impossible to hit all the objectives at the same time. Because they cannot achieve the impossible, policy makers generally settle for the lesser goal of 'trading-off' between policy objectives. A trade-off exists when two or more desirable objectives are mutually exclusive; success in achieving a particular objective or set of objectives is at the expense of a poor and deteriorating performance with regard to other policy objectives. **For the idea of a trade-off: up to 3 marks**

Over the years, UK macro-policy has been influenced and constrained by three significant policy trade-offs. The first trade-off has been between the 'internal' policy objectives of full employment and growth and the 'external' objective of achieving a satisfactory balance of payments (and possibly supporting a particular exchange rate). On many occasions, UK governments have used fiscal and monetary policy to expand demand in order to achieve full employment and economic growth. But as incomes grow, imports are drawn into the economy (via the marginal propensity to import), causing the balance of payments on current account to deteriorate. In order to reduce the payments deficit and/or to relieve speculative pressure on the pound's exchange rate, the government has to reverse policy and introduce tax and/or interest rate increases which deflate or contract the domestic economy.

Secondly, there has been the Phillips curve trade-off between full employment and the control of inflation. This is similar to the trade-off just described, but relates to the tendency for the rate of inflation to accelerate as a government expands demand in pursuit of full employment and growth.

Thirdly, governments may trade-off between the policy objectives of economic growth and a more equal distribution of income and wealth. During the Keynesian era, progressive taxation and transfers to the poor were used (as part of fiscal policy) to reduce inequalities between rich and poor. However, the pursuit of greater equality may have reduced the economy's growth rate and competitiveness. In recent years, free-market supply-side economists have argued that greater equality reduces entrepreneurial and personal incentives in the labour market, makes the economy less competitive and slows the growth rate. In the free-market view, greater inequalities are necessary to promote the conditions in which rapid and sustainable economic growth can take place.

For explaining a trade-off: up to 4 marks each, maximum of 7 marks

Examiner's tip

The key to answering this question is the concept of a policy 'trade-off', which is closely related to the fundamental economic principle of 'opportunity cost'. Your answer might also reflect what is sometimes known as the 'law of unintended consequences'. This law predicts that whenever the government intervenes in the market economy, effects will be unleashed which the policy makers had not foreseen or intended. Sometimes, government intervention can be justified on the grounds that the social benefits of intervention exceed the social costs and therefore contribute to a net gain in economic welfare. But if government activity, however well intentioned, triggers harmful consequences which are greater than the intended social benefits, then 'government failure' results.

---

2 Examiner's answer plan

(a) **(i)** Define inflation as a persistent and continuing tendency for the price level to rise. **Up to 2 marks**

(ii) Explain briefly how firstly excess demand and secondly 'cost-push' forces can cause inflation. **Up to 5 marks**

(iii) Indicate that in the past these have been regarded as alternative and competing explanations. **Up to 4 marks**

(iv) Go on to explain that they are now more usually regarded as complementary rather than competing explanations, i.e. indicate that you are agreeing with the statement in the question. **Up to 4 marks**

(b) Develop in some depth the implication that the government needs a 'many-pronged' strategy to counter and control inflationary pressures in the economy. **Up to 10 marks**

Examiner's tip

Until a few years ago, the 'demand-pull versus cost-push' debate dominated economists' discussion and analysis of inflation. As time went by, Keynesians drifted into the cost-push camp, while monetarists believed that inflation is purely a 'monetary phenomenon', always and only caused by growth of the money supply creating excess demand which pulls up the price level. In the 1970s and early 1980s, monetarists seemed to reject the possibility that institutional and structural factors such as the system of wage bargaining can cause cost-push inflation. The monetarist view was: 'governments cause inflation (by causing or allowing the money supply to expand); trade unions cause unemployment through the system of wage bargaining and the promotion of rigidities in the labour market'.

In recent years however, many Keynesians and monetarists have abandoned such extreme positions, adopting instead a more moderate or eclectic view similar to the statement in the question. According to this view, inflation gets into the system through excess demand in the upswing of the business cycle. Then, cost-push forces and an 'inflationary psychology' endemic in recent British economic behaviour maintains inflationary pressures well into the next recession, when the excess demand which initially triggered the inflation has dissipated.

The implication of the statement is that there is no single or simple solution to the problem of inflation. In recovery and 'boom' periods, the government must try to prevent too fast an expansion of demand, while during all the phases of the business cycle, including the recession, it should consider introducing appropriate supply-side policies to alter labour market and price-setting conditions and to change people's attitudes to inflation.

3 (a) The RPI is constructed by measuring the monthly changes in the prices of a sample of goods and services, selected to represent the expenditure pattern of a typical British family. Around the country, about 120,000 prices are noted each month for some 600 goods and services. Each item in the sample or national 'shopping basket' is given a 'weight' which is intended to measure the relative importance of the good in the pattern of expenditure for average families. For a chosen base year, the index number of every item in the sample (and of the whole of the RPI) is 100. When the price of a good in the sample rises in a subsequent month or year, this will be reflected in a higher index number for that good. Each good's new index number is multiplied by its 'weight', the totals are added and then divided by 1000 (the sum of the weights), to arrive at the RPI for the relevant month or year.

For construction: 2 marks

An economic index such as the RPI is only as good as the representativeness of the sample on which the index is based, and the accuracy of the weights granted to each item in the sample. Because people's spending patterns are constantly changing, the representative sample in the RPI will always be out of date to a greater or lesser extent, though regular revisions are made to update the sample. Likewise, the system of weights can never be completely accurate. Even if both sample and weights were accurate for a particular income group or household type, the RPI could never accurately measure how inflation affects income groups or household types (such as a low-income, single-person pensioner household) which depart significantly from the average. Every few years, the RPI needs to be 'rebased' to try to minimise the distorting effect of these problems.

For discussing problems: 2 marks

Examiner's tip

The question does not require a detailed explanation of how the RPI is constructed, but make sure you outline a selection of the 'representative sample', allocation of 'weights' to each item in the sample, the choice of a base year and finally, the need periodically to 'rebase' the RPI. State two problems (relating to the method of construction which you have described), but resist the temptation to overelaborate.

(b) (i) UK governments regard changes in the RPI as 'very important' for a number of reasons. Firstly, as with other examples of economic data, such as data series on unemployment and national output, the RPI provides the government with important information about what is going on in the UK economy. The government can base current and future economic policy on what is happening to the RPI (and other economic indicators). This has become especially important in recent years because the Conservative Government and the Bank of England have based macroeconomic policy on announcing, and then operating, policy so as to hit an inflation target, currently stated in terms of 'RPI – X', i.e. price changes as measured by the RPI but with mortgage interest payments excluded.

Secondly, movements in the RPI can influence people's 'inflationary expectations' either favourably or unfavourably. A sudden rise in the RPI may signal to people (perhaps falsely) that the government has lost control of the economy. This may then cause workers and firms to act in an inflationary way in their wage bargaining or price setting behaviour, bringing about exactly the situation the people had feared, a loss of control over inflation. Conversely, a rapid fall in inflation as measured by the RPI might cause people to reduce still

further their expectations of future inflation, thereby making it easier for the government to maintain its control over inflation.

Thirdly, the RPI is important for the government because significant elements of public expenditure are 'index-linked' to the RPI. For example, an increase in annual inflation as measured by the RPI automatically leads to an equal annual increase in nominal expenditure on state pensions and unemployment pay in order to maintain their real value.

For each reason: up to 3 marks, maximum of 4 marks

(ii) Trade unions can make use of information provided by the RPI when forming their wage claims, as can employers when deciding both their pay offers and their pricing strategies. Financial institutions such as building societies can try to attract savings by issuing index-linked securities (similar to the index-linked gilts and National Savings securities that the government has issued on occasion). Index-linked securities pay a much lower rate of interest each year than ordinary securities that are not index-linked. But they are still attractive to savers, particularly when the rate of inflation is both high and uncertain, because the capital or maturity value rises each year in line with the RPI, thus maintaining the security's real value.

For each use: up to 2 marks, maximum of 3 marks
Maximum of 5 marks overall

Examiner's tip

The mark allocation for this part of the question does not specify how the marks are divided between parts (i) and (ii). You will probably find it easier to develop your answer to part (i) rather than part (ii), but it is likely that the marking scheme is quite flexible. In your answer to part (ii) make sure you write about how the RPI can be of use to economic agents other than the government, for example firms, workers and consumers.

(c) According to the passage, the IFS report identified two reasons why the RPI overstates increases in the cost of living. The first point made is that goods and services whose prices have risen in the last year are 'over-represented' in the RPI's weighting system. This is because consumers respond to the price rises by switching their consumption towards cheaper substitutes. Since they buy *less* of a good whose price has risen, the weight allocated to the good in the index immediately becomes too great. Conversely, the weights allocated to the (now relatively cheaper) substitute goods become too small. As a result, the rise in the RPI overstates the true increase in average prices experienced by a typical household. Secondly, the IFS report argued that when firms increase prices because they have improved the quality of a good, the price rise should not be included in a measure of the rate of inflation. For example, when automobile manufacturers introduce new car models, the prices charged are usually significantly higher than those of the model range being replaced. However, new car models almost always embody technical improvements and a greater variety of features attractive to motorists. As a result, the price rise overstates the true increase in the cost of living.

For each weakness : up to 3 marks, maximum of 5 marks

Examiner's tip

This part of the question requires you to identify the weaknesses in the RPI, which (according to the IFS report) result in an overestimation of the rate of inflation. You should resist the temptation to discuss critically the points made in the report or to introduce any other factors which might offset these errors.

(d) Compared to the better-off and average income earners, lower income groups such as pensioners and the unemployed tend to buy relatively few consumer durable goods such as cameras and computers. The prices of these goods (which are largely imported from highly competitive Far-East sources), have often fallen in absolute as well as real terms in recent years, thereby depressing the overall RPI. By contrast, a relatively large proportion of the expenditure of the poor is for items such as home heating, public transport and council housing, whose prices have generally risen faster than the RPI.

If the RPI understates the true increase in the cost of living of low-income groups, this implies that the poor will gradually become even poorer relative to better-off households. Most low-income households (such as pensioners and the unemployed) receive part or all of their income from state welfare benefits which are index-linked to the RPI. To maintain their real purchasing power, the money value of these benefits would have to rise in line with the true increase in the cost of living of the poor. But, by increasing in line with the RPI instead, the real purchasing power of welfare benefits falls. Even if the RPI accurately measured the cost of living of low-income groups, these households would still find themselves sinking into relative poverty compared to people on average earnings. In most years, the real income and standard of living of wage and salary earners rises, largely due to increases in labour productivity. However, the index-linking of welfare benefits to the RPI (rather than to the index of average earnings) means that 'un-waged' benefit claimants are generally unable to share in the higher living standards enjoyed by the 'waged'.

For each reason: up to 3 marks, maximum of 6 marks

Examiner's tip

You must state at least one reason why the RPI may provide an incorrect measurement of changes in the cost of living of lower income groups. The conventional approach is to argue that the RPI understates the rise in the living costs of the poor. However, a more recent study, published by the Institute of Fiscal Studies in 1994, argues that the prices of necessities such as food, fuel and clothing have fallen in real terms since 1979, while the 'real' prices of 'luxuries' such as entertainment and services have risen. If this is true, then the RPI overstates inflation as it affects poorer households. In the 1994 report, the IFS calculated that in 1992, low-income families benefited from a cost of living increase 1 per cent below average, while the best-off suffered an inflation rate 3 per cent above average.

9 CONSUMPTION, SAVINGS AND INVESTMENT

Answer	Mark

1 Investment involves the purchase – usually by firms – of real resources which form part of the economy's capital stock and productive potential. Investment can be of two types: (i) investment in fixed capital such as new factories or plants, and social capital such as roads or publicly owned hospitals; and (ii) inventory investment in stocks of raw materials or variable capital. A country's gross investment includes two parts: replacement investment (or depreciation) which simply maintains the size of the existing capital stock by replacing worn-out capital, and net investment which adds to the capital stock, thereby increasing productive potential. **For definition: up to 8 marks**

In 1993, UK investment in fixed capital was about 15 per cent of total gross national product (GNP) in the economy, while inventory investment, which indicates whether firms are adding to or reducing their stocks of raw materials, was actually negative at under one per cent! Although the economy was recovering from recession, UK companies were failing to replenish the stocks of raw materials used up in the course of production. In any one year, the total stock or inventory of raw materials and finished goods which firms hold is about 40 per cent of national output. Current inventory investment simply adds to, or subtracts from, the total existing stock of inventories. In 1989, which was a 'boom' year, inventory investment had been about 5 per cent of final expenditure in the economy. By contrast, the negative investment in stocks of raw materials in 1993 reflects the fact that the UK economy was only just coming out of a recession and business confidence was still depressed. **Facts about investment: up to 8 marks**

There are a number of factors which influence the aggregate level of investment in the UK. These include: the relative prices of capital and labour, the nature of technical progress, the adequacy of financial institutions in the supply of investment funds, the impact of government policies and activities upon investment by the private sector, and the attractiveness of the UK as a site for inward investment undertaken by foreign multinational companies such as Japanese automobile manufacturers. The first and last of these factors are closely linked, since UK wage rates, which are relatively lower than those in many other EU countries, have been an important factor in attracting inward investment by Japanese and American companies, whose UK-located 'transplant' factories can now benefit from tariff-free access to a community market of over 400 million. Technical progress can influence the aggregate level of investment in many ways. By rendering existing capital equipment (such as computers) obsolete, technical progress can force businesses to invest in replacement capital. And by changing the nature of production towards more capital-intensive methods (as when automation replaces mechanisation), technical progress can add to the investment which firms must make in order to remain competitive. In the UK, the relatively low rate of investment in manufacturing capacity (compared to the UK's main competitors) has been blamed on the inadequacy of UK financial institutions, and also on government policy. Both have been accused of 'short-termism' and an unwillingness to finance or promote investment in major capital projects which could be profitable only in the long term. Government policy has been attacked from both the political left wing and right wing. From the left, Keynesians have argued that the level of investment reflects the inadequacy of government financial assistance to industry. Free-market critics on the right wing argue that the taxes and the public sector borrowing needed to finance excessive levels of public spending 'crowd out' private sector investment.

For listing factors: up to 5 marks each, maximum of 20 marks

In terms of theories of investment, the aggregate level of investment in the UK might be determined by the marginal efficiency of capital, the cost of borrowing or rate of interest, and the acceleration principle. The following diagram illustrates how the first two of these factors determine investment. The aggregate level of investment is determined at I_1, where the marginal efficiency of capital (shown by the curve MEC_1) equals the cost of borrowing. It would not be sensible for firms to undertake investment beyond this point. This is because the expected future productivity of any further investment project (the marginal efficiency of capital) would be less than the cost of borrowing undertaken to finance the project. Investment in such projects would not be consistent with profit-maximisation.

For developing a theory of investment: up to 30 marks each, maximum of 44 marks

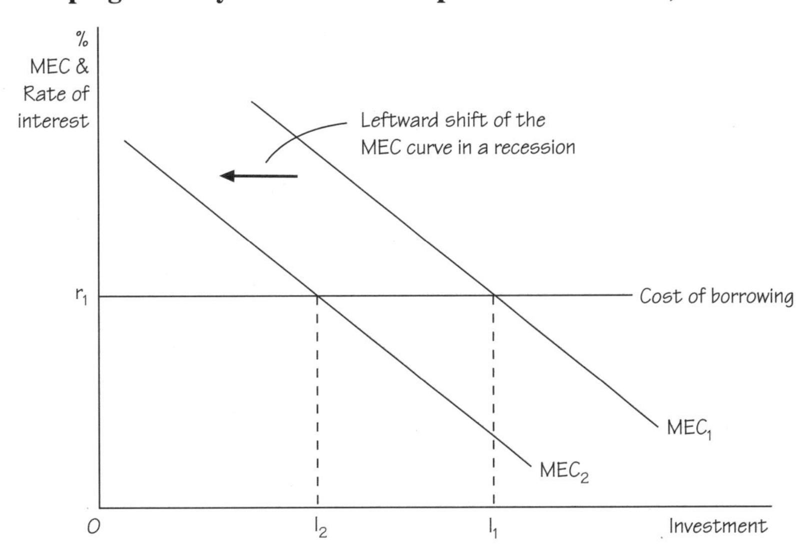

According to the acceleration principle, the level of aggregate investment can also be influenced by changes in the economy's rate of growth. Via the acceleration principle, an increase in the growth rate induces an absolute increase in investment, while a slowing down of growth causes a fall in the aggregate level of investment. As a result, the aggregate level of investment fluctuates more than the overall level of output or national income. This is consistent with the UK's experience in recent business cycles, with investment falling in the recession, but recovering in the subsequent upswing of the economy. The marginal efficiency of capital theory also contributes to the explanation of fluctuations in the aggregate level of investment in the UK. The position of the MEC curve depends in part upon the state of business confidence. In a recession, business confidence collapses, causing the MEC curve to shift leftwards to MEC_2. The aggregate level of investment falls from I_1 to I_2. When the economy and the state of business confidence recover, the MEC curve shifts rightwards again, increasing the level of aggregate investment. **For relating theory to evidence: up to 20 marks**

Examiner's tip

The wording of the question reflects the fact that a significant number of students taking A-level Economics are overseas students. The examination boards sometimes set questions which allow overseas candidates to illustrate their answers from the experience of their own countries. To earn a high mark on this question, you must cover at least two theories of investment, making sure you relate the theory to UK experience (unless of course you live outside the UK or have a reasonable knowledge of another country's economy).

2 Examiner's answer plan

(a) Briefly define the three concepts: consumption, income and investment.
1 mark each, maximum of 3 marks

(b) Introduce and briefly explain the Keynesian theory that consumption is determined by the level of income. Illustrate the relationship on a 45° line diagram. **Up to 4 marks**

(c) Explain how an upward shift of the consumption function (or a change in autonomous consumption) will also bring about a multiplier effect, causing national income to rise.
Up to 5 marks

(d) Draw an investment function on your diagram and explain the investment multiplier, whereby an increase in investment leads to a multiple increase in national income.
Up to 4 marks

(e) Explain how, via the accelerator principle, investment changes in response to a change in the level of income. **Up to 4 marks**

(f) Bring together the multiplier and accelerator principles, explaining how through their interaction, income, investment and consumption change over time. **Up to 5 marks**

Examiner's tip

This question tests a number of very important macroeconomic relationships. These are: (i) the autonomous consumption multiplier, which measures the effect upon national income of an upward or downward shift of the consumption function; (ii) the investment multiplier, which measures the effect of a change of investment upon income; (iii) the accelerator, whereby the level of investment responds to a change in the level of consumption and/or income; and (iv) the propensity to consume, which measures planned consumption at different levels of income. Given the 'disguised' nature of the question, it is possible to gain high marks by identifying only two of the four relationships, providing your answer shows a clear and confident understanding of each of the relationships identified.

---

3 (a) The personal saving ratio in Figure 1 measures personal saving as a ratio of total output (GDP) produced domestically in the economy. By contrast, the personal saving ratio in Figure 2 measures personal saving as a ratio of the disposable income of the personal sector. Personal sector disposable income is smaller than GDP (which includes the gross income of the corporate and government sectors as well as the personal sector), so a smaller denominator used in the calculation results in a larger ratio, for example 5% in Figure 2 for 1988 rather than the 3–4% shown in Figure 1.

For explaining that the two ratios measure different variables: up to 4 marks

Examiner's tip

Firstly, taking an illustrative year in the data series, identify the difference in the size of the two ratios. Then, explain the difference in the figures you have noted (clue: are the ratios measuring the same economic variables?).

(b) (i) There seems to be a slight increase in the corporate saving ratio from just under 10% to about 11 or 12 % of GDP. There are several possible explanations for this: the corporate sector may simply have grown and become a more significant part of the economy; the corporate sector might have become more profitable so that companies had more retained profits available to save; tax

changes may have encouraged companies to save. The data also shows company saving rising in the upswing of the business cycle and falling in the recession. This is probably explained by the availability of profits to save, though strictly this relates to cyclical variations around the trend rather than to the trend itself. **For explaining trend in corporate saving: up to 3 marks**

(ii) Government sector savings have fallen from about 8% of GDP in 1970 to about 3% in 1989, though this overall fall masks a more dramatic fall to a negative value (i.e. the government sector becoming a net dissaver) from 1977 to 1986, followed by a recovery in the government sector saving ratio after 1986. The fall in the government sector's saving in the first part of the period covered by the data is probably related to the worsening of the government's finances. These were years in which the government's budget deficit grew both in absolute size and as a proportion of GDP. Likewise, the later recovery in the government sector saving ratio can be explained by the improvement in the government's finances from 1987 to 1991, when the government's finances moved into surplus. As a result, the government did not need to borrow to finance a budget deficit. The data in Figure 1 ends in 1989 – presumably the government sector's saving ratio fell again over the next few years as the government's budget once again moved into deficit. **For explaining trend in government saving: up to 3 marks**

(iii) In the first and last years shown by the data, the personal saving ratio was around 5% of GDP, but as with the other two ratios, there was considerable fluctuation over the period. The main changes were the doubling of personal sector saving to over 10% of GDP in the mid-1970s, and the fall in the ratio to around 4% of GDP in 1988. The rise in the ratio occurred at a time of high inflation and negative real interest rates, which reduced the real value of households' accumulated stocks of saving. Households were forced to save more out of current income to try to restore the real value of their eroded wealth assets. Increased uncertainty induced by the high and variable inflation rate also contributed to the rise in the personal saving ratio. The fall in the personal saving ratio in the 1980s probably resulted from greater consumer confidence and feelings of certainty about the future, reinforced by the effects of financial deregulation and house price inflation. With house price inflation outstripping the general rate of inflation, owner-occupiers' real wealth increased, thereby reducing their need to save out of current income. Deregulation of the financial system in the mid-1980s greatly increased the supply of funds available for households to borrow, with financial institutions falling over themselves to lend on very easy terms to households.

For explaining trend in personal saving: up to 3 marks

Examiner's tip

To identify a trend in an economic variable, data covering more than one business cycle is usually necessary. Since the data in Figure 1 extends from 1970 to 1989, it should be possible to detect trends for corporate, government and personal sector saving. In each case, first quote a couple of statistics to illustrate the trend, and then offer at least one possible explanation of the trend you have identified. Note that savings by nationalised industries (or public corporations) are included along with saving by private sector companies (but not unincorporated businesses) in the corporate sector saving ratio. You might have expected the savings of nationalised industries to be a part of the government sector saving ratio. This adds to the difficulty of explaining the trends.

(c) The fall in the personal saving ratio meant that consumption increased as a proportion of personal sector disposable income. Provided that this increase was not offset by a fall in the expenditure of one of the other sectors of demand (as a result of an increase in the government or the corporate sector saving ratios), this would have had an immediate impact upon aggregate demand.

For relating saving to consumption: up to 2 marks

On the following Keynesian income/expenditure diagram, the fall in the saving ratio accompanied an upward shift of the consumption function from C_1 to C_2, and of the aggregate expenditure function from E_1 to E_2.

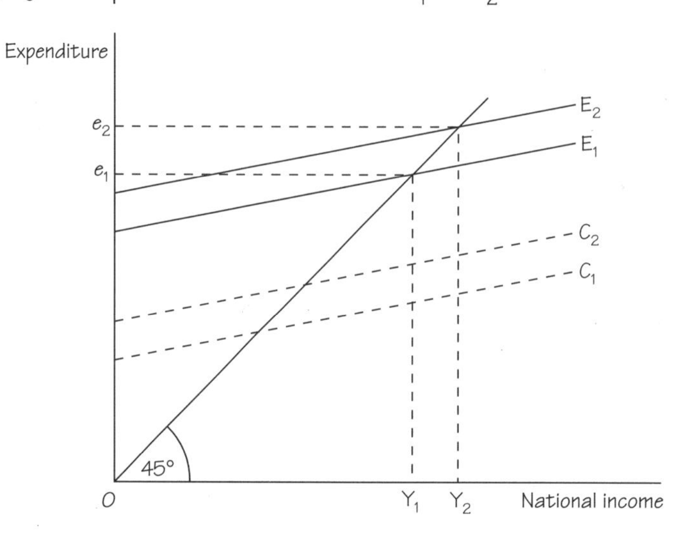

The diagram also illustrates the multiplier effect which occurred. The upward shift of the aggregate demand or expenditure curve from E_1 to E_2 increased national income from Y_1 to Y_2. At Y_2, aggregate expenditure is higher at E_2 than it would have been had the level of income remained at Y_1.

For using Keynesian theory to explain the effect on aggregate demand: up to 2 marks

Examiner's tip

State the obvious point that the increase in consumption (which is the obverse of the fall in the saving ratio) will increase the level of aggregate demand, shifting the aggregate demand (AD) curve rightwards. Then go on to explain how this leads to a multiplier effect which further stimulates income and demand.

(d) In part, the answer to this question is simply the reverse of the answer to part (c). A rise in the personal saving ratio accompanies a fall in consumption, which induces a multiplier effect whereby the level of output and activity falls by a greater amount than the initial decrease in consumption. Thus, if the economy is already entering a recession (because, for example, a collapse of business confidence has reduced investment), a rise in the personal saving ratio will add to the downward pressures on economic activity. **For relating saving to consumption: up to 2 marks**

Recovery from recession obviously becomes easier if consumer confidence returns and consumers start spending rather than saving. Indeed, in recent British business cycles (up to but not including the recovery from the recession of 1990–92), a fall in the personal saving ratio and an increase in consumption was a vital ingredient in bringing the economy out of recession. The recovery phase of the UK business cycle tended to be 'consumption-led' rather than 'export-led' or

'investment-led'. But, while consumer spending can undoubtedly lift an economy out of recession, it may be incompatible with sustainable economic growth, unless accompanied by increased investment and exports. The recovery taking place from recession in the early and mid-1990s may be more sustainable, precisely because investment and export demand have lifted the economy, with the saving ratio remaining high and consumer spending flat. In contrast to past consumption-led recoveries, the recent recovery may have equipped the UK economy with a more efficient and competitive industrial base, without the growth of income dissipating into rising prices and an import spending spree that would render the recovery unsustainable. **For relating to the business cycle: up to 2 marks**

Maximum of 3 marks overall

Examiner's tip

Relate the rise in the personal saving ratio to a change in the level of aggregate demand, and then go on to discuss how the multiplier process affects national income and employment. Explain how the rise in the personal saving ratio deepens (and perhaps even causes) the recession, and then make the point that recovery from a recession is more difficult (though not impossible) with a high personal saving ratio.

10 TAXATION, GOVERNMENT SPENDING AND THE PSBR

Answer	Mark

1 The reduction in the standard and top rates of income tax that took place during the 1980s reflected the supply-side fiscal policy that the Conservative Government introduced during these years. Indeed, the Government hoped to go further; by 1990 it had announced the medium-term objective of reducing the standard rate to 20% 'as soon as it is prudently possible'. And although the budgets of 1993 and 1994 raised the general level of taxation, the Government increased the tax burden without increasing the marginal rates at which income tax is levied.

For providing relevant background to the tax changes: up to 15 marks

The Government believed that the reductions in income tax rates would improve labour market incentives and increase the economy's supply potential and total output. For this to happen, the supply curve of labour must be upward-sloping, as shown in the left-hand panel of the diagram overleaf. In this situation, a cut in the marginal rate of income tax (being equivalent to a rise in the hourly wage rate from W_1 to W_2) leads to an increase in supply of labour from L_1 to L_2. With employment, incomes and output growing in response to the labour market incentives, the government eventually ends up collecting more revenue from income tax, despite the lower tax rates. The government's tax take might be further increased if workers and entrepreneurs who engaged in tax avoidance and evasion at the previously 'penal' tax rates, now decide that these practices are not worthwhile.

For relating the tax changes to the government's intentions: up to 10 marks

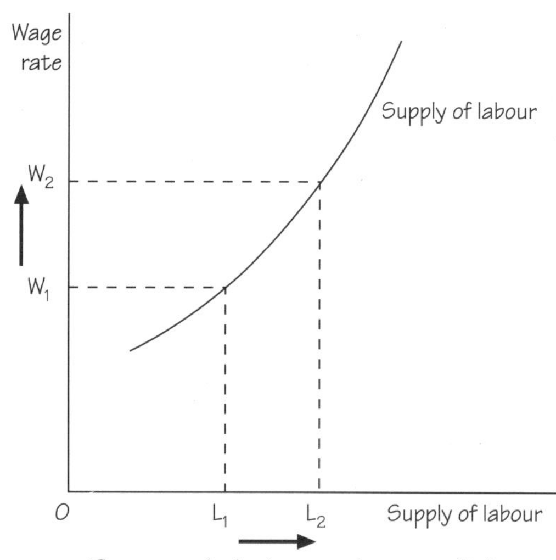

The upward-sloping supply curve of labour

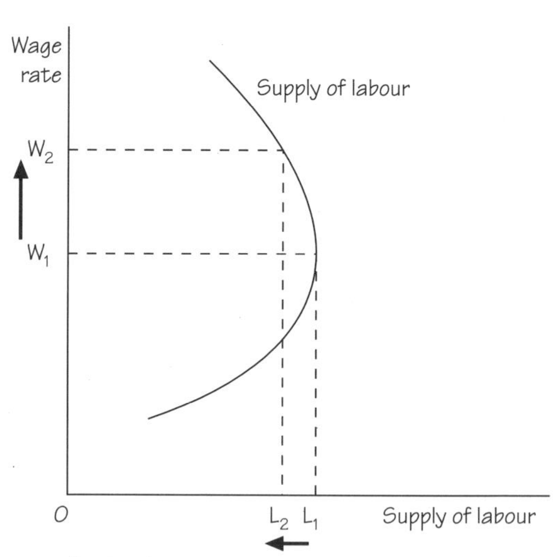

The backward-bending supply curve of labour

But if the supply curve of labour is backward-bending – as in the right-hand panel of the diagram, the consequences could be different. Workers and entrepreneurs might respond to the tax cuts by working less hard, choosing to enjoy more leisure time rather than to supply extra labour and effort.

For brief statement of a possible consequence: up to 10 marks each, maximum of 30 marks

There might be three further consequences of the income tax cuts. Firstly, the cuts in the marginal rates at which income tax is levied tend to shift the structure of taxation away from taxation of income and towards the taxing of expenditure. This shift would occur even if the rates at which indirect taxes on expenditure are levied were left unchanged. But if at the same time as cutting income tax rates, the Government were to raise expenditure taxes, for example by increasing the standard rate of VAT or by extending the tax base to include domestic fuel and lighting, the shift to expenditure taxation would be even more marked.

This shift from direct to indirect taxation might not occur if the Government fails in subsequent years to raise tax thresholds in line with inflation, or if it abolishes or reduces income tax allowances such as the mortgage interest allowance. In a process known as 'fiscal drag', a failure to raise tax thresholds in line with inflation drags people into the tax net. More of people's income ends up being taxed and the resulting higher average rates of income tax might actually increase the burden of income tax, despite the lower marginal tax rates.

Secondly, and partly because of the shift just noted, the tax changes have made the tax system significantly more regressive and contributed to increased poverty. Before the tax changes, the income tax structure was more progressive, taking a significantly larger proportion of the income of the better-off. Expenditure taxes are generally regressive, falling more heavily upon the poor than on the rich as a proportion of income. Because the reductions in the marginal rates of income tax, particularly the higher rates, have been combined with increases in expenditure taxes, the effect has been doubly regressive. Indeed, when the effects of cuts in the real and relative value of welfare benefits and wage reductions for low-income earners are also taken into account, the changes in the tax system have contributed to a growing inequality between rich and poor.

Thirdly, when the Conservative Government introduced these tax cuts, it promised, partly for political reasons, that it would never raise income tax rates. If this is true,

the Government has abandoned the use of fiscal policy to manage aggregate demand, Keynesian-style. This may have left the government in the 'one club golfer' position of having just one policy instrument (interest rates) available for short-term intervention in the economy. **For further development of consequences: up to 15 marks each**

Maximum of 45 marks

Examiner's tip

You should clearly relate the standard and top rates of income tax to the concept of the marginal tax rate. Indicate that the changes in these rates which are quoted in the question consequently reduce the extent to which the UK income tax structure is progressive. Although the question does not mention expenditure (or indirect) taxes, you should make (and possibly expand) the point that the consequences of the changes in the marginal rates at which income tax is levied will depend in part on any changes simultaneously being made to the structure of indirect taxation. Note also the use of the word *likely* in the question. This suggests that you should forecast consequences which have not yet occurred – it is perfectly valid to forecast the future (providing your forecasts are based on sound economics). It is equally valid to answer the question by quoting changes which
sound economics). It is equally valid to answer the question by quoting changes which
have already occurred in the UK economy (providing they occurred after the last year quoted in the question, 1990) arguing that the changes or events you mention were the consequences of the tax changes.

---

2 Public expenditure can be defined as spending undertaken by central government, local government or public authorities such as public corporations and 'quangos' – quasi-autonomous non governmental organisations such as the Arts Council and the English Tourist Board. In the financial year 1994/95, general government spending (the spending of central and local government) had risen to about 45 per cent of GDP (from a low of 39.75 per cent in 1989/90), though the government hopes to reduce the proportion back towards 40 per cent by the year 2000. **For definition: up to 3 marks**

Both the level and the pattern of public spending are partly the result of current and recent government policies and decisions, partly the result of government policies and decisions made many years ago, and partly the result of changes taking place autonomously in the economy, over which the government has little if any control.

For identifying relevant factors: up to 3 marks each, maximum of 9 marks

Taking the latter first, both long-term demographic (population) changes and shorter-term changes related to the business cycle have significant effects on the level and pattern of public expenditure. In the UK, the increase in the number of old people, particularly the very old, has been the most significant demographic change affecting public expenditure. Public spending on retirement pensions and health care have both increased. These are examples of 'demand-led' public spending. Past legislation has granted people rights to state pensions and to health care provided by the National Health Service. As the population ages, more people take up these rights, so increased demand raises the level of public spending and changes its pattern.

Unemployment benefit (now called 'job-seeker's allowance') provides another example of demand-led public spending. Public spending on unemployment benefit and related benefits has tended to rise because of long-term structural changes taking place in the economy which have increased unemployment. Public spending on unemployment benefits also varies with the business cycle, increasing in a recession but falling in the recovery phase of the cycle. The growth in demand-led public spending on unemployment benefit provides the main explanation for the rise in the level of public spending in the early

1990s when the UK economy suffered a severe recession. Likewise, providing economic recovery continues through the rest of the decade, falling expenditure on welfare benefits should cause the level of public expenditure to fall as a ratio of GDP.

Discretionary government decisions, as well as *autonomous* changes which are outside the government's control, can also affect both the level and the pattern of public expenditure. In the past, governments have made decisions to provide through public spending, goods and services which had previously only been available through private sector market provision. The decisions to provide free state education and health care (as merit goods) or roads (as a public good) obviously raised significantly the overall level of public spending and changed its pattern. In recent years, however, the main thrust of government policy in the UK has been in the opposite direction: to reduce rather than to extend public sector provision of goods and services, and state provision of welfare benefits or transfers. Decisions to raise prescription charges or to abolish free eye tests have reduced public expenditure on health care. And while the government decision to increase the number of 18-year-olds in universities has increased public spending on education, the decision to replace student grants with student loans has worked in the opposite direction. The policy of privatising nationalised industries has reduced public spending, since the government does not subsidise industries it no longer owns. Likewise, a policy of privatising motorways (with their new private owners charging tolls) would reduce public spending. But because of the autonomous changes taking place in the economy mentioned already, policy decisions such as these are unlikely to reduce the overall level of spending significantly, though they may nibble at the edges and account for some changes in its pattern.

For relevant development of a factor: up to 6 marks each, maximum of 13 marks
Maximum of 25 marks overall (17 marks if answer is restricted to either pattern or level)

Examiner's tip

The pattern and the level of public expenditure are closely related. A factor which is responsible for changing the pattern may also change the level and vice versa. Make sure you don't confuse 'public expenditure' with 'expenditure by the general public', i.e. consumption spending. In the UK, recent changes in public spending reflect to some extent the Conservative Government's attempt to reduce the overall level of public expenditure (albeit not necessarily successful) through policies such as privatisation and marketisation.

---

3 Examiner's answer plan

(a) Define the Public Sector Borrowing Requirement as the flow of net new borrowing undertaken by the whole of the public sector (not just central government) to finance the difference between public sector expenditure and revenue. When revenue exceeds expenditure, surplus revenue can be used to repay previously accumulated debt: the Public Sector Debt Repayment. **Up to 3 marks**

(b) Explain: (i) that a Keynesian government may deliberately run a budget deficit to inject demand into the economy; (ii) how the public sector's deficit and borrowing requirement rises cyclically in a recession; (iii) that the PSBR may increase because the government has lost control of its finances. **3 × 1 mark**

(c) Explain that because the economy was enjoying an economic boom, total tax revenues were rising despite cuts in direct tax rates. A shift from direct to indirect taxation had also taken place. Both public spending increases and debt repayment could be financed out of buoyant tax revenues. **2 × 2 marks**

(d) (i) Explain how tax revenues fall, and demand-led spending on unemployment benefits rises, as output falls and unemployment increases in a recession. **Up to 3 marks**

(ii) For this part of the question, you must use the data. The graph shows that the public sector's finances were already in severe deficit before 1981, but were in significant surplus immediately before 1991. In both 1981 and 1991, the public sector's finances deteriorated, with the relative deterioration being greater in the 1990s recession. **Up to 3 marks**

(iii) The fact (already explained) that the public sector's finances automatically deteriorate in a recession accounts for the similarity; differences can be explained in terms of the state of the finances immediately prior to the recessions, and in terms of the government's reaction to the deterioration. In the earlier recession, the government introduced quite severe cuts in public spending which reduced the PSBR, whereas by the early 1990s, the government had accepted once again the Keynesian argument that the PSBR should be allowed to grow in a recession, functioning as an 'automatic stabiliser' to dampen the fluctuations in the business cycle. The government also deliberately expanded the economy prior to the 1992 general election, whereas it had resisted this temptation before the 1983 election.
Up to 2 marks per similarity or difference, maximum of 4 marks

Examiner's tip

There are a number of short questions to answer here, each carrying only a few marks. Do not 'overwrite' your answers by going into lengthy explanations. Keep your answers short and to the point. The question also states that the recession which hit the UK economy in the early 1980s began in 1981. The recession actually began earlier than this (in 1979), reaching a trough in 1981, with output beginning to recover in 1982.

11 MONETARY POLICY AND FISCAL POLICY

Answer **Mark**

1 (a) The use of monetary policy to control the growth of the money supply is associated with the term 'monetarism'. According to monetarist theory, inflation is caused by a prior increase in the money supply. Monetarists therefore argue that if the rate of growth of the stock of money in the economy (or money supply) can be reduced, the rate of inflation will fall. **For basic statement: up to 5 marks**

In the late 1970s and the early 1980s, UK monetary policy was indeed based on this simple logic. In 1980, the Conservative Government introduced the Medium Term Financial Strategy (MTFS) to 'plot the path for bringing inflation down through a steady reduction in the rate of growth of the money supply secured by the necessary fiscal policies'. The objective of the MTFS was to bring about a gradual reduction in the growth of money GDP (or the nominal value of domestic output) whilst leaving the growth of real GDP unaffected, in the belief that this would result in lower inflation. Central to the strategy in the monetarist period of the early 1980s, was the announcement of medium-term targets for the growth of the money supply, designed to 'talk-down' the rate of inflation by causing workers and firms to reduce their inflationary expectations. The monetarists argued that if people believe that a tough government means business in sticking to its monetary

targets and reducing inflation, they will immediately begin to behave in a less-inflationary way, which in itself will reduce inflation!

For relevant development: up to 20 marks

When the policy of controlling the money supply was actually implemented, a number of significant problems arose, which forced the authorities to abandon the policy in the mid-1980s. In the first place, the authorities cannot exercise direct control over most of the money supply, which takes the form of bank deposits and other liabilities of the private enterprise financial and banking system. While the authorities can exercise indirect control over the growth of the money supply in principle (using monetary policy instruments such as open market operations and interest rates), this control can never be complete. It follows that published money supply targets can seldom be hit with complete accuracy. This leads to a second problem with money supply targets. Monetarists argue that an important ingredient for a policy's success is its credibility. The credibility of the money supply targets is vital if people's inflationary expectations are to be lowered. Failure to hit a pre-announced money supply target can destroy the government's credibility, which in turn may affect expectations adversely and – even worse – lead workers and firms to conclude that the government has lost control over the economy!

For explaining problems of controlling the money supply: up to 20 marks

A third problem which arises when attempting to control the money supply relates to what is known as 'Goodhart's Law'. This law is named after Charles Goodhart, currently a professor at the London School of Economics, who was a Bank of England official in the 1970s. Goodhart's Law states that as soon as a government tries to control the growth of a particular measure of the money such as M4, any previously stable relationship between the targeted measure of money and the economy will break down. According to Goodhart, this is because the more successful a monetarist government appears to be in controlling the rate of growth of the financial assets which it defines as the money supply, the more likely it is that other financial assets, regarded previously as 'near monies' outside the existing definition and system of control, will take on the function of a medium of exchange and become money. Goodhart's Law thus has the significant implication for monetarism that, by its nature, money is a 'will-o'-the wisp' that cannot be controlled. Essentially, 'money is as money does'. Any attempt at controlling the growth of the money supply is likely to be cosmetic. The authorities may succeed in controlling what they define as money, but by that time, other financial assets will have become money, rendering the control ineffective.

In summary, the three problems outlined above support the case that monetary policy should not be based on controlling the growth of the money supply, though it may be argued that monetary policy and control of inflation should both be at the heart of the government's macroeconomic policy. **For conclusion: up to 15 marks**

Examiner's tip

Controlling the money supply is closely associated with monetarism. There are two ways in which you could approach this question. On the one hand you might debate whether economic policy in general, and monetary policy in particular, should be based on monetarist theories, or whether a Keynesian approach to managing the economy is more appropriate. Alternatively, you might accept the monetarist propositions, that monetary policy should be central to macroeconomic policy and that its prime objective should be the control of inflation. In this case, discuss whether control of the money supply is the most appropriate intermediate objective of a broadly 'monetarist' monetary policy.

(b) The first of the two problems I am going to discuss was significant from the mid-1980s until 1992, when the exchange rate replaced the money supply as the central target of UK monetary policy. During the latter part of this period, the pound's exchange rate was fixed at a high parity against other European Union currencies within the Exchange Rate Mechanism (ERM) of the European Monetary System. The strategy was based on the theory that a high exchange rate can reduce inflation. The policy of targeting the exchange rate did indeed reduce inflation, but at the cost of the long and deep recession suffered by the UK economy during the years of ERM membership. **For stating problem: up to 4 marks**

Arguably, the pound entered the ERM in 1990 at an overvalued rate, which rendered UK exports uncompetitive in world markets. As a result, the balance of payments on current account deteriorated and the UK monetary authorities were forced to support the exchange rate by raising interest rates to prevent a speculative flow of capital out of the pound. Because the rate of interest was assigned to supporting the overvalued exchange rate, the cost of borrowing could not be lowered to stimulate demand in order to ease the UK economy out of recession. This was the main problem encountered in the operation of monetary policy in the UK in the early 1990s. **For relevant discussion: up to 16 marks**

A second problem, the credibility of monetary policy (referred to earlier, in the context of controlling the money supply), has been very significant in recent years. Credibility disappeared almost completely when the pound's exchange rate was fixed in the ERM. Although the Conservative Government announced that monetary policy would continue to support a fixed exchange rate, most people believed the issue was *when* the exchange rate would be devalued, not *if*. Eventually a massive speculative run against the pound occurred which forced the pound out of the ERM and brought to an end the role of the exchange rate as the central objective of monetary policy. **For stating second problem: up to 4 marks**

The problem of maintaining credibility has continued to plague monetary policy since the pound's exit from the ERM. In 1992, the Government gave the Bank of England greater freedom to raise or lower interest rates in the effort to hit the explicit inflation rate target which replaced the exchange rate as the focus of monetary policy. In theory, this gives financial markets greater confidence that the Government will not meddle in the setting of interest rates in order to gain a short-term political advantage. However, it now seems evident that as a general election approaches, the Government is finding it difficult to resist the temptation to override the Bank of England, thus threatening once again to destroy the credibility of the strategy at the heart of its monetary policy.

For relevant discussion: up to 16 marks

Examiner's tip

The question gives you plenty of scope for choice here. If you choose examples of problems which affect all types of economic policy (such as fiscal policy) as well as monetary policy, make sure to restrict your answer to discussing how the problem has affected monetary policy in recent years. Examples of such problems include the unreliability of the statistical information on which policy must be based, the effect of time lags in the implementation of policy, the effect of policy trade-offs, and the problem of maintaining the credibility of the policy. Alternatively, you might identify and discuss problems which have arisen as the targeting of monetary growth has given way to the targeting of the exchange rate firstly, and then to an explicit inflation rate target as the central plank of monetary policy. But do not go back too far; the question relates to the last ten years.

2 Monetary policy can be defined as that part of a government's overall economic policy through which the government tries to achieve its objectives, whatever they may be, by using monetary instruments such as controls on bank lending and the raising or lowering of interest rates. Likewise, fiscal policy is the part of government policy which uses fiscal instruments (altering the structure and rates of taxation, public spending and the public sector's budgetary position) to achieve the government's policy objectives. Fiscal policy and monetary policy may be assigned to different policy objectives; alternatively they may be used to support each other or even to achieve the same objective, such as the management of aggregate demand.

For defining each policy: up to 3 marks each, maximum of 5 marks
For clarity of the distinction: up to 3 marks

During the Keynesian era (from the 1950s to the 1970s), fiscal policy was indeed associated primarily with the management of aggregate demand. However, since the end of the Keynesian era in the late 1970s, monetarist-inspired governments have generally rejected the use of taxation and public spending as discretionary instruments of demand management. Monetarists argue that when fiscal policy is used to stimulate or reflate aggregate demand in order to achieve growth and full employment, the policy will be at best ineffective, and at worst damaging. Any growth of output and employment will be short-lived, and, in the long term, the main effect will be to accelerate inflation, thereby destroying the conditions necessary for satisfactory market performance and 'wealth creation'.

A monetarist government would subordinate fiscal policy to the needs of monetary policy. Monetarists believe that control of public spending and the PSBR (in the government's fiscal policy) is a necessary precondition for successful control of the money supply (in monetary policy). Instead of using fiscal policy to manage demand, a 'monetarist' government might base policy on a medium-term fiscal 'rule' to reduce public spending, taxation and government borrowing as proportions of national output. Besides reducing the inflationary effects of 'big government spending', such a fiscal policy should prevent public spending 'crowding-out' the private sector. Monetarists believe that public sector spending and borrowing crowd-out the private sector in two ways. 'Resource crowding-out' occurs when the government uses resources in its public spending programme which might otherwise have been employed in private sector production. Secondly, 'financial crowding-out' occurs when the government borrows to finance public sector spending. An increase in the PSBR causes interest rates to rise, which increases the cost of investment finance for the private sector. **Up to 8 marks**

As well as adopting a fiscal policy which is consistent with the monetary policy aim of controlling inflation, monetarists recommend that the macroeconomic elements of fiscal policy should also be subordinated to a more microeconomic fiscal policy based on tax cuts to create incentives to work, save and to be entrepreneurial. Monetarists and supply-side economists believe that workers respond to cuts in income tax rates by working harder. Conversely, high rates of income tax and a high overall tax burden create disincentives which, by reducing national income as taxation increases, also reduces the government's total tax revenue. The Laffer curve opposite shows how the government's total tax revenue changes as the average tax rate increases from zero to 100 per cent. Tax revenue must of course be zero when the average tax rate is zero per cent, but the diagram shows that total tax revenue is also zero when the tax rate is 100 per cent. This is because with an average tax rate set at 100 per cent, all income must be paid to the government as tax. In this situation, there would be no incentive to produce output other than for subsistence, so with no output being produced, the government would end up collecting no tax revenue! Between these limiting rates of zero and 100 per cent,

the Laffer curve shows tax revenue first rising and then falling as the average rate of taxation increases. Tax revenue is maximised at the highest point on the Laffer curve, beyond which any further increase in the average tax rate becomes counterproductive, causing total tax revenue to fall. **Up to 6 marks**

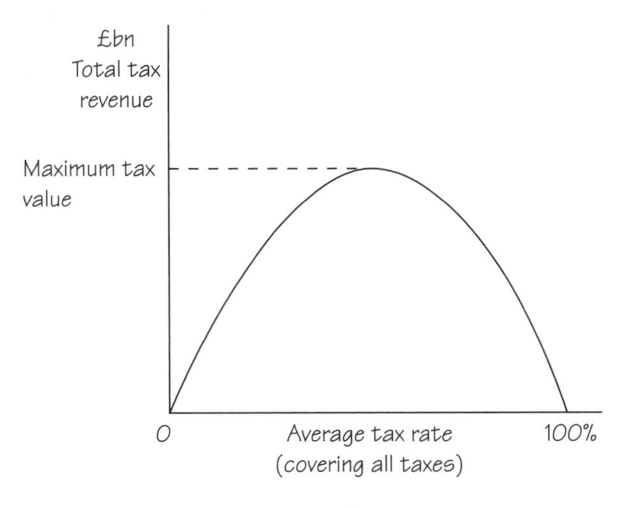

A Laffer curve

Monetarists and supply-side economists argue that the increase in the tax burden in the Keynesian era, which was required to finance a growing government sector, raised the average tax rate towards or beyond the critical point on the Laffer curve at which tax revenue is maximised. In this situation, any further tax increases would have the perverse effect of reducing the government's total tax revenue still further. Indeed, tax cuts rather than tax increases may raise total tax revenue, since a growing national output, stimulated by lower tax rates, will yield higher total revenue despite the reduced tax rates. The effect would be reinforced by a decline in tax evasion and avoidance, as these activities become less worthwhile at less 'penal' tax rates.

Given that governments have to levy taxes to raise revenue to finance necessary government expenditure, monetarists believe that the structure or pattern of taxation should be switched away from taxes on income and capital and towards taxation of expenditure. All taxes are, of course, unpopular and resisted to some extent by taxpayers, but some are more unpopular than others. Supply-siders believe that expenditure taxes are less unpopular than income tax, and therefore more acceptable to taxpayers. Although initially disliked when first imposed or when tax rates are raised, expenditure taxes are less 'visible' than income taxes. Taxpayers soon get used to expenditure taxes and learn to live with them. Monetarists also argue that expenditure taxes have a further significant advantage. Unlike income taxes, expenditure taxes do not have a substitution effect which distorts the choice between labour and leisure, a distortion which supply-siders believe operates against the supply of labour and in favour of not working. Indeed, in so far as expenditure taxes – like all taxes – introduce some distortion into the economic system, they do so by raising the price of consumer goods, which encourages households to substitute saving in place of consumption. This is an important virtue in the monetarist and supply-side view of the world.

Up to a further 3 marks

Examiner's tip

There is a danger of answering this question much too narrowly, by defining monetary policy solely in terms of monetarism and fiscal policy in terms of Keynesian demand management. This could mean that when answering the second part of the question, you would argue (wrongly) that, because monetarists reject Keynesian demand management, they don't support the use of any type of fiscal policy!

---

3 Examiner's answer plan

(a) (i) Define the nominal interest rate as the money paid in interest on a loan over a time period such as a year, expressed as a ratio of the total amount owed. **Up to 2 marks**

(ii) Then go on to define the inflation rate as the change in the average price level between two years, expressed as a ratio of the price level in the first of the two years. **Up to 2 marks**

(b) Explain that a number of factors determine interest rates, including risk, the liquidity of the loan, the margin between the rates at which financial institutions borrow and lend, etc. Then develop your answer by explaining with examples that these vary for different loans and result in different interest rates. For example, unsecured loans are more risky than secured loans, so carry a higher rate of interest. **Up to 4 marks**

(c) Explain how a fall in nominal interest rates increases demand, possibly leading to demand-pull inflation. This outcome depends upon the initial state of the economy, for example whether or not the economy is operating significantly below capacity, exhibiting an 'output gap'. Explain also that the reduction in nominal interest rates should reduce cost-push inflationary pressures, particularly if firms' real cost of borrowing falls. **Up to 4 marks**

(d) (i) Outline a monetary measure such as contractionary open market operations or the imposition of controls on bank lending. **Up to 2 marks**

(ii) Then move on to fiscal policy, outlining how tax increases and public spending cuts may reduce inflation by deflating demand. **Up to 4 marks**

(e) (i) Explain that the real rate of interest is the nominal rate of interest minus the rate of inflation. Explain that according to the data, the nominal interest rate was 12.5 per cent at the beginning of April 1991 while the inflation rate was 6.4 per cent. **Up to 2 marks**

(ii) Having performed the necessary calculation, go on to explain how the real rate of interest (rather than the nominal rate) indicates whether savers earn a real return on the amount they have earned and whether borrowers are incurring a real cost from their indebtedness. For example, for savers to earn a real return which increases the real value of their wealth, the real rate of interest must be positive. **Up to 2 marks**

(f) (i) Explain that higher real rates of interest in the UK would raise businesses' real costs of production, thereby reducing the UK growth rate. **Up to 4 marks**

(ii) Then go on to explain how higher real interest rates attract short-term capital flows into the UK, which improve the capital account of the balance of payments. However, by raising the exchange rate to a higher level than would be the case with lower real interest rates, trade competitiveness would be further reduced. The current account might well deteriorate, though you should note that higher interest rates depress aggregate demand and reduce imports, a factor which tends to improve the current account. **Up to 4 marks**

Examiner's tip

This is another example of a data question made up of many parts, each carrying just two or four marks. Be careful not to overwrite your answers, but do note which parts of the question require an element of explanation as well as definition. Also be careful to avoid misinterpreting part (c) of the question. Don't write about how the inflation rate affects interest rates. The question asks about the reverse relationship, the effect of changes in the (nominal) interest rate upon inflation. When calculating the real rate of interest in part (e), make sure you show the method of calculation used. Finally, in your answer to part (e), list and briefly explain at least two effects that higher real interest rates have upon both growth and the balance of payments.

12 INTERNATIONAL ECONOMIC ISSUES

Answer	Mark

1 (a) Before explaining and illustrating how the principle of comparative advantage can work to make trade efficient, I will first define the key concepts in the question, 'efficiency' and 'comparative advantage'. Efficiency has a number of meanings in economics, but in the context of this question, efficiency can be defined in terms of the world economy's production possibility frontier. An outward movement of the production possibility frontier from PP_1 to PP_2 represents a gain in efficiency, provided the outward movement results from increased output being produced from the same total resources. **For defining concepts: up to 5 marks**

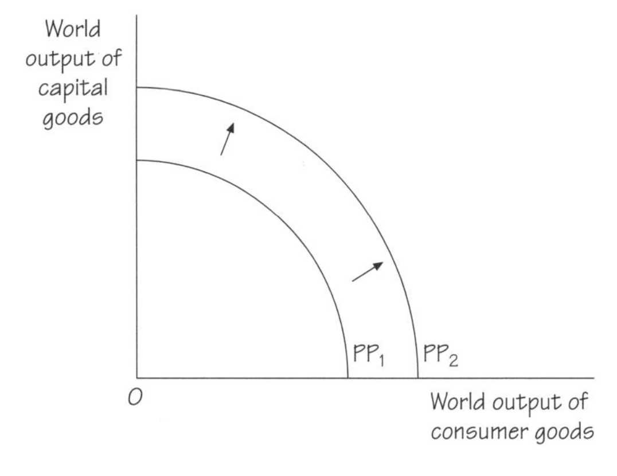

The second key concept in the question, comparative advantage, must not be confused with absolute advantage. A country possesses an absolute advantage in producing a good or service if it can produce more of the good from given factors of production or inputs than any of its competitors. Comparative advantage, by contrast, is measured by what a country gives up in terms of other goods, when it produces a particular good or service. The country which gives up the least other goods when it increases production of a particular good, possesses the comparative advantage in that good. As the following numerical example shows, it is quite possible for a country to have an absolute disadvantage in the production of a good, while still enjoying a comparative advantage.

To illustrate the principle of comparative advantage, and to explain how the principle can work to make trade efficient, I have constructed a simplified model of the 'world' economy, by assuming just two countries, Atlantis and Pacifica, each with just two units of resource (for example man-years of labour) that can produce just two commodities, guns or butter.

Each unit of resource, or indeed a fraction of each unit (because I am assuming that resources or inputs are divisible), can be switched from one industry to another if so desired in each country. Suppose that in each country the production possibilities are such that one unit of resource can produce:

In Atlantis: 4 guns or 2 tons of butter
In Pacifica: 1 gun or 1 ton of butter

Quite clearly, in terms of technical efficiency, Atlantis is 'best at' – or has an absolute advantage in – producing both guns and butter, but it only possesses a comparative advantage in gun production. The opportunity cost of producing one extra gun in Atlantis is half a ton of butter sacrificed, whereas Pacifica would have to forego a whole ton of butter. But what about butter production? When increasing its butter output by one ton, Atlantis gives up two guns. By contrast, Pacifica would only have to give up one gun to produce an extra ton of butter. Thus Pacifica possesses a comparative advantage in butter production even though it has an absolute disadvantage in both products.

When one country possesses an absolute advantage in both industries, as in the example above, its comparative advantage will always lie in producing the good in which its absolute advantage is greatest. Similarly, the country that is absolutely worst at both activities will possess a comparative advantage in the industry in which its absolute disadvantage is least.

For developing the model of comparative advantage: up to 7 marks

Developing the model a little further will show that specialisation, in accordance with the principle of comparative advantage, can lead to a gains in total output, and hence to an efficiency gain. If no specialisation occurs and each country devotes one unit of resource to each industry, total production will be:

5 guns and 3 tons of butter

Now if each country completely specialises in producing the good in which it possesses a comparative advantage, total production becomes:

8 guns and 2 tons of butter

With *complete* specialisation, production of one good (guns) has risen, production of the other (butter) has fallen, which does not represent a net gain in output. However, it is possible to devise a system of *partial* specialisation which will meet the condition for an efficiency gain: specialisation should result in at least as much of one good and more of the other, compared to when there is no specialisation. For example, Pacifica could completely specialise, but Atlantis could devote just enough resources (half a unit) to 'top up' butter production from 2 to 3 tons. Atlantis's remaining one and a half units of resource could then be directed into gun production to produce 6 guns. Total production would now be:

6 guns and 3 tons of butter

Since at least as much butter and more guns are now produced compared to the earlier 'self-sufficient' situation, quite clearly specialisation in accordance with the principle of comparative advantage has led to an increased output and hence an efficiency gain.

For further relevant development: up to 3 marks

Examiner's tip

It is possible to interpret the key instruction to 'illustrate' in more than one way. You could provide a numerical example of comparative advantage in tabular form, or you could base your illustration on graphs showing two countries' production possibilities for two goods. Whichever method of illustration you choose, it is important to explain carefully how your example illustrates comparative advantage and to use your example to explain how an efficiency gain can result from specialisation in accordance with the principle. Include one or other of the concepts of technical, productive or Pareto efficiency in your answer.

(b) A number of economic arguments (as well as political, military and social arguments) are used to justify protectionism. Developing countries argue an economic case for import controls to protect 'infant industries' from established rivals in advanced economies while the infant industries develop full economies of scale. The opposite economic case is sometimes made in advanced industrial economies such as the UK to protect 'sunset' or 'geriatric' industries (such as coal mining) in the older industrial regions from the competition exercised by newer industries in developing countries. Both arguments are really special cases of a more general argument in favour of protectionism: that import controls are justified, at least on a temporary basis, to minimise the social and economic costs of the painful adjustment process as the structure of an economy alters in response to either changing demand or to changing technology and comparative advantage. In recent years, Keynesian economists have sometimes advocated the selective use of import controls in the macroeconomic management of the economy. They regard import controls as a potentially effective supply-side policy instrument, to be used either in place of or in addition to traditional demand-side Keynesian policies. These controls could be used to prevent unnecessary deindustrialisation and to allow orderly rather than disruptive structural change in the manufacturing base of the economy. **For setting out reasons: up to 7 marks**

At a more deep-seated level, the economic justification of protectionism stems from the proposition that the model of comparative advantage is based on unrealistic assumptions, and that as soon as more realistic assumptions are made, the case for free trade becomes much weaker. The model of comparative advantage assumes that factors of production are both immobile between countries and instantly switchable between industries. Protectionism is justified on the basis that neither of these assumptions is true in the real world. On this basis, trade unions argue that import controls are necessary to prevent multi-national firms shifting their capital to the low-wage conditions of developing countries and exporting their output back to the countries from which the capital was moved. They further argue the case for employing labour, however inefficiently, in protected industries rather than allowing labour to suffer the greatest inefficiency of all: mass unemployment. Also, the model of comparative advantage I developed assumes constant returns to scale. But in the real world, increasing returns to scale or decreasing returns to scale are both possible and indeed likely. In a world of increasing returns, the more a country specialises in a particular industry, the more efficient it becomes, thereby increasing its comparative advantage. This argument can be used to support the case (mentioned earlier) for protecting infant industries in developing countries until they also have built up economies of scale and can compete 'on a level playing field' with established large firms in First-World countries. But if decreasing returns to scale occur, specialisation erodes efficiency and destroys the initial comparative advantage. A good example occurs in agriculture when over-specialisation results in

monoculture, in which the growing of a single cash crop for export may lead to soil erosion, vulnerability to pests and falling agricultural yields in the future.

Finally, a case for protectionism stems from the fact that the comparative advantage model ignores the possibility that over-specialisation may cause a country to become particularly vulnerable to sudden changes in demand or to changes in the cost and availability of imported raw materials or energy. Changes in costs, new inventions and technical progress can eliminate a country's comparative advantage. The principle of comparative advantage implicitly assumes relatively stable demand and cost conditions. The greater the uncertainty about the future, the weaker the case for complete specialisation. Indeed, if a country is self-sufficient in all important respects, it is effectively neutralised against the danger of importing recession and unemployment from the rest of the world if international demand collapses. **For further development of reasons: up to 3 marks**

Examiner's tip

This question requires you to identify, and then to explain briefly, a number of economic arguments to justify import controls and at least some restriction on the freedom of world trade. Beware of straying into non-economic arguments, such as the desire to be self-sufficient in military weapons or the ethical decision to refuse to trade with undemocratic political regimes. The question does not require you to assess whether the economic case for protectionism is stronger than the case for free trade, but you should indicate whether you think that the reasons you introduce into your answer have any merit.

---

2 Examiner's answer plan

(a) (i) Briefly explain the meaning of the current account. **Up to 2 marks**

(ii) Define a current account deficit in terms of the monetary value of visible and invisible trade imports exceeding the monetary value of exports. Illustrate with an example taken from recent UK experience. **Up to 4 marks**

(b) (i) Explain why a current account deficit is usually regarded as a problem, emphasising the point that a large and persistent deficit reflects the uncompetitiveness of the country's exports. **Up to 8 marks**

(ii) Explain that the extent to which a deficit should be regarded as a problem depends on the exchange rate regime. In theory, a floating exchange rate should restore competitiveness and a deficit should not be a serious problem for the government. But with a fixed exchange rate, a deficit may pose significant problems if the exchange rate is overvalued and if the rules of the exchange rate system do not permit the country to devalue to restore competitiveness. Illustrate your answer from Britain's experience in the ERM. **Up to 3 marks**

(iii) Explain how the current account can be affected by the state of aggregate demand in the domestic economy. In the upswing of the business cycle, buoyant demand 'sucks' imports into the economy, causing the current account deficit to grow, but depressed demand reduces the deficit in the downswing. This means that a deficit is less of a problem in the recovery period of the cycle, provided the deficit is expected to disappear in the subsequent recession. But if the current account remains significantly in deficit throughout a recession, this indicates that the country's exports are uncompetitive in world markets and/or that the exchange rate is overvalued. **Up to 3 marks**

Examiner's tip

The question asks only about the current account of the balance of payments, so it is irrelevant to introduce the capital account, except perhaps to explain that the problems caused by a current account deficit may be made worse by any destabilising 'hot money' flows induced by the deficit. The question was inspired by the fact that the UK current account remained in significant deficit throughout the recession which hit the British economy in the early 1990s. It would therefore be useful, though not essential, to illustrate the points you make from UK experience, particularly with regard to the effect of ERM membership on both the economy and the state of the current account.

---

3 (a) (i) 'Visible trade' is trade in goods which have to be physically transported between two countries. The 'balance of visible trade' is a measure of the monetary value of exported goods minus the monetary value of imported goods for a particular time period – quarterly data is shown in the diagram. 'Invisible trade' involves services rather than goods, and other items such as profit flows between countries and expenditure by tourists. The 'balance of invisible trade' measures the monetary value of invisible exports minus the monetary value of invisible imports for a particular time period. **Up to 3 marks**

(ii) It is difficult to identify a trend from the data, because the data is restricted to one business cycle. To be more confident of identifying a long-term trend, I would need data which covered at least two successive business cycles. A *feature* of the data (but not necessarily a trend) is that the balance of visible trade is in deficit throughout the period covered by the data, while invisibles are almost always in surplus. Over the whole period, the invisible surplus seems to be getting smaller. Visible trade and the overall current account (which is the addition of the visible and invisible balances), vary with the phases of the business cycle; the deficit being greatest when the economy is booming, but shrinking in periods of recession. **For description: up to 3 marks**

The cyclical nature of the visible balance and the overall current account can be explained by variations in the overall level of aggregate demand in the different phases of the business cycle. When the economy is doing well in the upswing of the cycle, buoyant levels of aggregate demand draw imports into the economy, via the marginal propensity to import. Thus the trade balance deteriorates. Conversely, during a recession, the fall in the demand for imported goods results from the depressed state of aggregate demand in the economy.

For account: up to 3 marks
Maximum of 5 marks for part (ii)

Examiner's tip

The first part of the question simply requires definitions and a distinction between the balances of visible and invisible trade; you don't have to describe what the data shows or perform any calculations based on the data. Briefly describe the trend in your answer to the second part, but devote most of your answer to accounting for the trend you have identified. Be careful not to overwrite your answer – there are only 5 marks available in total!

(b) (i) As indicated in the answer to part (a), the main changes in the current account probably relate to the business cycle. The current account deteriorated between 1987 and the middle of 1989 as the UK economy

experienced a boom (growing from an exact 'balance' at the end of the first quarter of 1987 to a deficit of over £6bn by the third quarter of 1989), with the deficit shrinking in the subsequent recession to less than £1bn in the second quarter of 1991. The deficit then began to grow again, even though the UK economy was still in deep recession. However, changes in the exchange rate and interest rates (base rates) would have had some effect on the current account, both directly and also indirectly via their effects on the business cycle. For example, the increase in interest rates shown by the data between 1987 and 1990 eventually helped to force the economy into recession, which reduced the size of the current account deficit.

For identifying relationships: up to 3 marks

With regard to the exchange rate, the years from 1987 to 1991 covered the period when the monetary authorities were 'shadowing the Deutschmark', and then the two years during which the pound's exchange rate was fixed at a high parity within the ERM. The authorities deliberately raised interest rates to engineer a rise in, and then support, the exchange rate. The data in Table 1 shows that the exchange rate appreciated by over 5 per cent between 1987 and 1988, before falling back nearer to its 1987 parity. Despite this fall, the exchange rate was probably overvalued throughout these years in terms of the international trading competitiveness of UK exports, given the fact that the UK inflation rate was rising in the boom and exceeded that of Britain's main competitors. An overvalued exchange rate, propped up by high UK interest rates, may explain why the current account remained in deficit in the depths of a deep recession. **For explaining relationships: up to 3 marks**

(ii) Speculative capital movements or 'hot money' flows in the capital account of the balance of payments were an important factor influencing bank base rates during this period. A speculative flow out of the pound (or even the possibility of such a flow) would cause the monetary authorities to raise the Bank of England's lending rate in order to support the exchange rate, triggering a general increase in sterling interest rates. Other factors influencing base rates might be the effects of financial deregulation which increased the competition for banking business, and the inflation rate. Other things being equal, base rates tend to rise when inflation increases, partly to restore the real return on savings. **1 mark per factor, maximum of 2 marks**

Examiner's tip

For the first part of this question, you must first identify relationships, and then offer at least one explanation for each relationship identified. Remember, it may be a two-way process: for example, a deterioration in the current account may cause the exchange rate to change, which in turn could 'feed back' to affect the current account. For the second part of the question, mention at least two factors and provide a very brief explanation of how they may affect bank base rates.

(c) As already noted, from 1990 to 1992 the pound's exchange rate was fixed against other member currencies within the Exchange Rate Mechanism (ERM) of the European Monetary System. When joining the ERM in 1990, the Conservative Government made the decision to fix the pound at a high rather than a low parity, largely because (at the time), a high exchange rate played a key role as the intermediate monetary target in the Government's counter-inflation strategy.

For relating the data to the decision to join the ERM: 1 mark

The high exchange rate reduced the competitiveness of British exports and contributed to the fact that the current account remained in deficit. As a result, high interest rates were needed to support the pound as the exchange rate came under speculative pressure. Taken together, all these factors certainly lengthened and deepened the recession which hit the UK economy in 1990, even though they were probably not the immediate cause of the recession. Despite its intentions, the Government could not maintain the high fixed exchange rate. Following intense speculative pressure and the failure of a massive interest rate rise to head off a run on the pound, the fixed exchange rate was abandoned in September 1992, since when the exchange rate has floated. Table 2 shows that the sterling index (which measures the pound's value against a 'basket' of about 16 leading trading currencies) fell from 92.0 in August 1992 to 78.3 by November 1992, a devaluation of over 14 per cent. The immediate reason for the fall in the pound's value lay in the fact that the monetary authorities were no longer prepared to support the pound's exchange rate within the ERM by using up reserves to purchase the pound and setting interest rates at the high level needed to stem a capital outflow. Additionally, the authorities decided to alter the whole strategy of monetary policy, allowing the pound to freely float and market forces to take the exchange rate down to the level needed to restore the competitiveness of UK exports. A floating exchange rate allowed the authorities to set monetary policy and interest rates with the needs of the domestic economy in mind. Hence the Bank of England deliberately reduced its lending rate (thus causing the fall in the commercial banks' base rates shown in the table) in order to stimulate domestic demand and lift the economy out of the deep recession.

For relating the data to the economic situation after leaving the ERM: up to 3 marks

Examiner's tip

This is a 'disguised' question testing your knowledge of the fact that the rate at which the pound was fixed within the ERM came under increasing speculative pressure in the early autumn of 1992, before being forced out of the fixed exchange rate system on 'Black Wednesday' in September 1992.

The author and publishers gratefully acknowledge the following for permission to use questions, text and figures in this book:

Questions

Questions 1, 2 (Unit 1); 3 (Unit 2); 2, 3 (Unit 3); 1 (Unit 4); 1 (Unit 5); 3 (Unit 6); 2 (Unit 8); 2 (Unit 9); 2 (Unit 10); and 2 (Unit 11): Reproduced by kind permission of the Associated Examining Board. Any answers or hints on answers are the sole responsibility of the author and have not been provided or approved by the Board. Questions 2 (Unit 2); 3 (Unit 4); and 2 (Unit 5): Reproduced by permission of the University of Cambridge Local Examinations Syndicate. The University of Cambridge Local Examinations Syndicate bears no responsibility for the example answers to questions taken from its past question papers which are contained in this publication. Questions 2 (Unit 4); 2 (Unit 7); 1, 3 (Unit 9); 1 (Unit 10); 1 (Unit 11); and 3 (Unit 12): Reproduced by kind permission of the University of London Examinations and Assessment Council. The University of London Examinations and Assessment Council accepts no responsibility what so ever for the accuracy or method of working in the answers given. Question 1 (Unit 7): Reproduced by kind permission of the Northern Examinations and Assessment Board. The author accepts responsibility for answers provided, which may not necessarily constitute the only possible solutions. Questions 2 (Unit 6) and 2 (Unit 12): Reproduced by kind permission of the University of Oxford Delegacy of Local Examinations. Questions 3 (Unit 8) and 1 (Unit 12): Reproduced by kind permission of the Oxford and Cambridge Schools Examination Board. The answers are the responsibility of the author and have not been provided by the Board. Questions 3 (Unit 1); 1 (Unit 2); 3 (Unit 5); 1 (Unit 8); 3 (Unit 10); and 3 (Unit 11): Reproduced by kind permission of the Scottish Examination Board. Answers are the sole responsibility of the author and have not been provided by the Board. Questions 1 (Unit 3); 1 (Unit 6); and 3 (Unit 7): Reproduced by kind permission of the Welsh Joint Education Committee.

Text and figures

pp10–11 extract adapted from 'Competition and Innovation' by G.A. Geroski, Series Economic Papers no 71, October 1988, an internal economic paper for the Commission of the European Communities, reprinted by permission; p14 table from The Independent, 12 January 1994, reproduced by permission; p15 article adapted from 'Tunnel tariffs won't add up when the novelty wears off' by Ben Laurance, The Guardian, 12 January 1994, reprinted with permission; p18 table based on figures from Department of Employment Gazette, Employment Gazette, Annual Abstract of Statistics, British Business; pp24–5 article adapted from 'A market made out of muck' by Barbara Durr, Financial Times, 10 June 1992, reprinted with permission; p32 article adapted from *Discovering Economics*, edited by D Gray, Causeway Press Ltd, 1988, from 'The Cost of Living as Measured by the RPI', Joanna Slaugher, The Observer, 18 May 1986, reprinted by permission of Causeway Press Ltd and The Observer; p35 graphs reprinted from *Savings and Investment* by Christopher Pass and John Sparkes, Collins, reprinted by permission of the authors; p45 graph and p46 tables: from Economic Trends NoXX 1992. Central Statistical Office. Crown Copyright 1992. Reproduced by the permission of the Controller of HMSO and the Central Statistical Office.